THE MAKING OF THE GREAT COMMUNICATOR

Ronald Reagan's Transformation from Actor to Governor

KEN HOLDEN

LYONS PRESS
Guilford, Connecticut
An imprint of Globe Pequot Press

Copyright © 2013 by Kenneth Holden

Lyons Press is an imprint of Globe Pequot Press.

All photos courtesy of the author.

Project editor: Meredith Dias
Layout artist: Melissa Evarts

Library of Congress Cataloging-in-Publication Data is available on file.

ISBN 978-0-7627-7849-2

Printed in the United States of America

10 9 8 7 6 5 4 3 2 1

For Julie, gone these ten years, but always with me

"The men who succeed best in public life are those who take the risk of standing by their own convictions."

—JAMES A. GARFIELD,
IN A NOTE KEPT BY RONALD REAGAN

CONTENTS

Author's Note   xi

Prologue   xiii

Part One

1 A Star Is Born   3

2 The Gipper   13

3 The Speech   31

4 Behavior Modification   39

5 The Split   71

6 Stealth Campaign   97

7 The Candidate   101

8 The Blunder   109

9 The Call   119

10 The Meeting   131

Part Two

11 Day One   139

12 Day Two   149

13 Day Three   157

Part Three

14 The Fourth Day   167

15 The Circuit   173

16 On the Road   187

17 A New Face   197

18 Answered Prayer   201

19 A Distraction   207

20 "I Am Not a Politician!"   217

21 New Agreement   223

22 And . . . Cut!   231

CONTENTS

Epilogue   239
Acknowledgments   243
Appendix: "A Time for Choosing"   245
Bibliography   259
Index   261

Author's Note

We had him for three days in a tiny beach cottage near Malibu. This was in early 1966. Just three of us in a small beach cottage. An unlikely candidate for governor of California, he'd already goofed up a few public appearances. He couldn't seem to get his footing, he looked unprepared, he mangled details. The men who had discovered him and fallen in love with his possibilities were blistering, ready to give up on him. Better a quick writeoff, they were saying. Better wait for the next guy.

But not us, not Stan Plog and I.

We saw right away that he had the goods. He just needed a little push, some direction, what you'd now call tweaking. And we were right. He had the gift. He understood immediately, with a kind of intuitive genius, what we were getting at: how to handle himself in front of a crowd, how to manage the press, how to deliver his answers in small, powerful doses. Like a thoroughbred reacting to a gentle touch, almost before the command, he would go where we were going before we had to tell him. He seemed to know before we did.

It was as if he were waiting for us.

Only three people on earth knew the full story of what happened in Malibu over those seventy-two hours, how we helped transform a B-movie actor into a political giant. That's not too much to claim. His movie career was washed up, and he had limited range on television. But he did have something else. White-hot fire burned inside the man, and he viscerally understood that—under the right circumstances—he could connect powerfully with the American people. It was something to see, this priceless candidate being born. When it all came together, when the magic kicked in, it was as if the public had been waiting for him, just as he had been waiting for us.

Ronald Reagan died in 2004, and Stan Plog is just gone, in 2010, so only I'm left standing. I know the full story. I'm the only one left to bear witness.

Prologue

Pictures filled the house. Well, this was the home of a movie star. The walls glittered with the long, loving memories of his career: Duke Wayne, Doris Day, Robert Taylor, Pat O'Brien, George Murphy, Jack Benny—all smiling their movie-star smiles at us, all with heartfelt dedications to "Dear Ronnie," "My great pal, Ron," "Ronnie, a man's man!"

Stan and I were a little awestruck. In early 1966, we were two still-young academics and pioneers in the infant field of behavioral psychology, new to the sharp end of politics. Nevertheless and underneath it all—unbeknownst even to ourselves—we were ready for a firefight.

Nancy met us at the door, with that irresistible, soft, sunny smile, welcoming us to her home.

"Did you have trouble finding it?" she asked.

Pacific Palisades was an enviable location, an ideal destination for successful people, halfway between Santa Monica and Malibu, near the coast. No, it wasn't hard to find—just hard to imagine.

"Can I get you something? Please, make yourselves comfortable."

Out of a perfect picture window lay a faultless green golf course, and on the other side of the room, out another window, the azure beauty of the Pacific Ocean. It was a handsome house, an impressive house, a movie star's house. A grand piano held court in the living room, and on it sat a picture of William Holden (no relation, as far as I know). He had been the best man at Ron and Nancy's wedding in 1952. It was casually impressive—not showy—and it let you know exactly who you were dealing with.

"He's been a little under the weather. Nothing serious, a slight infection."

She took us into the den, a cozy room with a cowboy motif. Big bookcases lined the walls, filled with serious books, about Jefferson, Madison, Adams, and Tom Paine; volumes about Lincoln and Theodore Roosevelt; whole stretches of philosophy: Plato, Aristotle, and Locke. It was a thinking man's library.

"Does he read all these books?"

"Oh, yes, he's up late at night, reading, reading, reading."

Two other guys, both in their forties, were waiting in the den. Lyn Nofziger, the press secretary, an old newspaper hound sporting a sloppy Van Dyke beard—his Mickey Mouse tie half blown and a portable typewriter perched on his lap—had a cigar dangling out of his mouth. He had a friendly but careful smile. He was our friend.

Sprawled on the couch was Bill Roberts, the high-priced campaign consultant. Not a dumpy bag of laundry like Nofziger, but expensively rumpled and quietly bad-tempered. He muttered a greeting. Not our friend.

The introductions were unnecessary, but a certain formality obtained.

"Stan Plog and Ken Holden, Lyn Nofziger and Bill Roberts."

The meeting had taken only a day to arrange—lightning speed in a matter of this scope, but the rush was imperative. This was a true crisis. Everyone knew that the stakes couldn't be higher. So decks were magically cleared, schedules quickly rearranged. The money guys didn't dither, not when it came to the whole ball game.

Nancy stepped out of the room for a second. Roberts was muttering something that sounded like a complaint. Nofziger was chuckling to himself, probably enjoying one of his own bad puns or even worse jokes.

Suddenly everything stopped. We turned, and there he was, standing in the doorway in his casual sports jacket, his perfectly pressed slacks, and his dazzling shy smile: Ronald Reagan. He lit up the room, and we knew exactly why we were there.

PART ONE

1

A Star Is Born

Just a month after that introduction in Pacific Palisades, we spent our weekend in Malibu, where Stan and I worked with Ronald Reagan to get him started on the road that would take him through the Republican primary contest, then on to Sacramento as California's governor, and eventually to Washington as the nation's fortieth president, and into the history books. We were among the first pebbles in a landslide that swept the country and changed the world.

But to get to that weekend in Malibu, you have to retrace three pathways, the three very different lives that converged with just one great mission in mind. We were, all three of us, Midwesterners who had followed various dreams to California. We'll get to Stan's story and mine, but first we need to consider the extraordinary man whose life and ambition brought us all together—Ronald Reagan.

Reagan's official birth date is February 6, 1911, but he could have been a day older. His mother, Nelle Reagan, a quiet, deeply religious Protestant, had to endure a grueling and seemingly endless labor in a five-room apartment above a row of shops in Tampico, Illinois, before her son made his grand entrance.

In the middle of her great ordeal, her husband, Jack Reagan, a big, hard-drinking Irish Catholic, went to fetch a doctor. When the ten-pound baby boy finally arrived—a full twenty-four hours after the labor began—it was with such a howling clamor that his father laughingly bestowed upon him the affectionate nickname that clung throughout his life: "For such a little bit of a fat Dutchman, he makes a hell of a lot of noise, doesn't he?"

Thus, "Dutch" was born.

His mother took a sunnier view of the whole thing: "I think he's wonderful," she said.

At least that was the way that Dutch remembered it in his memoir, *Where's the Rest of Me?* His brother, Neil—nicknamed "Moon" because he parted his hair down the middle like the comic book character Moon Mullins—was three years older and viewed the new arrival with a mixture of suspicion and competitive envy. He had been shuttled off to live with neighbors during the transition and naturally harbored some sibling resentment.

An outgoing, gregarious person, Neil attempted to explain the shadings of personality that come down from parents and affect children beyond childhood. He was his father's son, he would say, for good or ill. His father was gregarious and charming, though by turns moody and pessimistic. Dutch, however, according to Moon, was his mother's darling and received her unqualified love and lavish praise. It was inevitable that Dutch forever viewed the world through the rosy lens of sheer optimism and complete self-confidence.

That difference colored their fates growing up. Moon hung out in the pool room and played cards at the fire station with his father's rough blue-collar friends, while Dutch stayed home taking elocution lessons from his mother.

Nelle was the descendant of Scottish and English Protestants. Reagan's paternal grandparents, Irish Catholic immigrants, hailed from Tipperary in southern Ireland. Driven to America by famine and ambition, the two clans eventually wound up in northern

Illinois, scratching out a working-class version of the American dream.

But in 1904, when the auburn-haired Nelle Wilson, a milliner, first set eyes on tall, dark Jack Reagan, the dissimilarity between their backgrounds only made him more attractive. He was a slick twenty-year-old shoe salesman with the gift of gab, she a twenty-one-year-old seamstress with a weakness for such a handsome youth with a smooth line. They also were both drawn to the charms of the theater.

They married in the Fulton, Illinois, Catholic church on November 8, 1904, but the issue of religion remained unresolved between them. Although she kept her promise to baptize Neil in the Catholic Church, by the time Ronnie came along she had joined the Disciples of Christ, an austere offshoot of Presbyterianism. It was in that particular Protestant church that the children all went to worship twice a week.

Jack Reagan had a problem: He drank too much. At first, Nelle tolerated his weekend and holiday binges. After all, he was a salesman and had to cultivate that social side of his life in order to do business. They still had strong ties to each other then, their shared affection for the stage high on the list. They joined amateur theatrical companies and held rehearsals in their home, sessions witnessed from a discreet distance with affectionate approval by the two young sons, both of whom gravitated in one way or another to the performing arts.

But Jack was feckless and footloose and heading down the slope to alcoholism. The Reagans began moving from town to town. Between the ages of six and ten, Dutch attended a different school every year. The family, Garry Wills wrote in *Reagan's America*, lived in five places in one small town, four in another, two in a third, "all rented; always living from suitcases, like actors." Dutch and Moon never had a real boyhood home.

In 1919, the family alighted once more in Tampico, where Ron had been born, to live above the H. C. Pitney Variety Store, where Jack worked. Then came Prohibition, which closed the town's one saloon. It wasn't enough to keep Jack on the wagon. A determined drunk didn't have to look too hard to maintain an alcohol habit, especially in Chicago where Jack went on his buying trips. His traveling and his drinking took a toll on the marriage. His drinking binges grew more frequent. His ambition to become financially independent—to own his own high-end fancy shoe store—evaporated, and the family fortunes fell like a stone. When the Pitney store went out of business in 1920, they moved one last time, to Dixon, Illinois.

Jack had somehow persuaded Mr. Pitney, his employer, to sell his store and invest in a shoe store in Dixon. He advertised that his store, Reagan's Fashion Boot Shop, was better than the other four shoe stores in the town of a little over 8,000. His store had X-ray machines to better measure a customer's foot size. Jack was also calling himself a "graduate practipedist" because he had a correspondence degree from something called the American School of Practipedics, a semiscientific method of assessing the bones of the foot. The school from which Jack received his diploma was founded by none other than Dr. William Scholl, the original Dr. Scholl whose name lives on foot care products to this day.

The store got off to a bad start, though, and Jack continued his slide, aided by Dixon's many speakeasies. Yet it survived somehow, before the Depression finally did it in, in 1930.

Dutch thrived despite his tempestuous home life. He had a winning personality and a willing attitude. His photographic memory impressed his teachers, and he even skipped a grade. There were, however, shocking moments that suggest that the havoc of his father's alcoholism had a deeper impact than he let on. One day, in the winter of 1922, when he was eleven, he came home and found Jack unconscious on the snow-covered lawn. Dutch managed to get Jack to bed without alerting his mother.

It was a turning point. Within a few months, Dutch switched from Catholicism to the Disciples of Christ, his mother's faith. The Disciples—who gave the United States three presidents: Reagan, Lyndon Johnson, and James Garfield, the only minister ever elected to the nation's highest office—were ardent prohibitionists. For the rest of his life, Ronald Reagan was a careful and modest drinker.

But then he was always like that: outwardly withheld, almost shy, but inwardly steely and determined. He didn't show his wounds in public, yet he harbored a deep sympathy for the downtrodden. He grasped that everyone ran into a share of speed bumps in life and the only important thing was to deal with the problems and, if possible, maintain an upbeat attitude. Neil—ever his father's son—showed a more defiant side to the world. He converted back to his father's Catholic faith when he turned eighteen.

Meanwhile, their mother became more deeply involved in church affairs. The Disciples of Christ, founded just after the start of the nineteenth century, espoused an optimistic, uniquely American world view. They opposed slavery and promoted temperance. They believed in capitalism and middle-class virtues, particularly hard work. Success was to be admired, and it came to those who worked hard, lived right, and didn't waste their money. As Reagan later quoted Nelle, "All things were part of God's plan, even the most disheartening setbacks, and in the end, everything worked out for the best."

According to Bob Colacello's *Ronnie and Nancy*, Nelle and Ronnie took to visiting prisoners in the county jail, organizing sing-alongs, giving readings, and, according to Neil, "driving the sheriff nuts" with the pressure of their good deeds. Once a month Nelle and Dutch entertained the patients at Dixon State Hospital with banjo playing and recitals of improving works.

Nelle also fought openly against racial prejudice. Remember, the Disciples of Christ had opposed slavery in the previous century. In a town that hosted Ku Klux Klan parades, she brought black families home for dinner. Neil remembered sitting in the segregated, "colored," section of the movie theater. Young Ron taught Sunday school and preached tolerance and "clean speech, clean sports, clean living, and clean scholarship." Jack, for all his personal weaknesses, felt the same way, forbidding the kids to see D. W. Griffith's *Birth of a Nation* because it glorified the Klan.

If it was a hectic life, it diverted Ron's attention from all of their domestic woes. He joined the North Dixon High School Drama Club and was baptized into the Dixon Christian Church, where he taught Sunday school and sang in the choir. He developed his first crush, on Margaret Cleaver, a classmate and the daughter of his minister, the Rev. Ben Cleaver.

Above all, though, there was in Ronald Reagan a persistent drive, an ambition to succeed, a need to break away. Coupled with the habits of thrift that came of necessity and the homegrown appreciation of responsibility and effort, it made for a powerful engine. One result of their unsteady youth was that both brothers developed a healthy work ethic. Neil went to work at a cement company while Dutch spent the summer of 1926 as a construction worker making thirty-five cents an hour. The job gave him the added advantage of developing him physically: Reagan put some muscle on his thin frame.

But it took more than one job to keep the family afloat. Reagan had been caddying throughout junior high and high school, and it was on the golf course that he had his first brush with what we now call networking, coming under the patronage of important men. The trait came naturally to him, and over the years he cultivated it into a fine art. One of the first for whom he caddied was Charles Walgreen, who became America's premier drugstore tycoon.

Walgreen, the son of Swedish immigrants named Oloffson (as with many an immigrant, their Old World surname didn't survive the transition to America), was an example of the kind of American striver that Reagan learned to look up to. Born in 1873, he had been fired from his first job as a drugstore helper because he refused to shovel snow. But after serving in the Army during the Spanish-American War, he trained as a pharmacist and went to work in a drugstore in Chicago. When the owner retired in 1902, Walgreen bought the store—and another, and another, until by 1916 he had the beginnings of the nationwide chain we see today. Walgreen was an innovator: His stores carried non-pharmaceutical items, as well as the medicines that his pharmacists mixed in large batches and sold for less than his competitors. Walgreens opened low-cost lunch counters, built an ice cream factory, and, if you really want to give him credit for something world-changing, introduced America to the malted milk shake in 1927. For that alone, he has pride of place on my list of personal heroes.

If you're looking for coincidence—of the "Gee, isn't it a small world?" kind—there's also this little footnote: One of Walgreen's franchisees was Hubert Humphrey's father.

But there were other lessons to be learned from Walgreen. For one thing, he was fiercely anti-Communist. For another, he was a man of impressive generosity. When he died in 1939, the $500,000 from his life insurance policy went to a pension plan for his employees.

So, here were seeds planted: Communism was a blight on the world and needed to be confronted and ground under, and capitalism as practiced in America was a force that led people to better lives, whether as business magnates like Walgreen, giving of their largesse to help others, or as his employees benefiting from that open-handedness to ease their children onto the next rung of the ladder.

But of all the jobs Ronnie held during his teenage years, the one that mattered most, the one he counted with greatest pride, was as a lifeguard at Lowell Park on the Rock River. He worked from Memorial Day to Labor Day, from ten in the morning until ten at night, and he saved seventy-seven lives. That number comes both from Reagan's count and contemporary newspaper reports. There's actually a story that the Rock River number is seventy-eight; once, when Reagan returned to visit, his replacement had to take a bathroom break, leaving Reagan to keep an eye on the river—and he saved yet another flailing swimmer.

There were stories later of other lives saved, including one when he was fifty-six and governor of California and someone went under in a pool in Sacramento. So the real number hovers somewhere around eighty. After one particularly dramatic rescue, Reagan's picture made the front page of the local newspaper. It was a convincing portrait of an American hero.

Later in life, when he let his hair down and reminisced about his youth and his early influences, he said it was the rescues on the Rock River that instilled the most self-confidence—and gave him the most profound respect for human life and dignity.

However, according to Paul Kengor's splendid book, *The Crusader: Ronald Reagan and the Fall of Communism*, there was another, harsher lesson to be learned on the banks of the Rock River: Don't expect gratitude, even if you've just saved someone's life.

"Most, in fact, never thanked Reagan," Kengor writes. "Some were too embarrassed, especially the guys, who usually only thanked him grudgingly at the urging of girlfriends. He came to learn that many people seemed to hate being saved. 'Almost every one of them,' he claimed, 'later sought me out and angrily denounced me for dragging them to shore. "I would have been fine if you'd let me alone."'"

Later, he wrote in his autobiography, "Lifeguarding provides one of the best vantage points in the world to learn about people."

So, on the banks of the Rock River, two more strands weave into

Ronald Reagan's personality in the making. One is that, over and over again, he can save lives; he's confident in his own powers, and he has the courage to use them. He continued to do so in the face of indifference, ingratitude, and even outright hostility. Fast forward to the 1980s, widen the lens's focus from a swirling riverbank in prewar Illinois to a worldwide battle against the Evil Empire, as he dubbed it, and tell me you don't see the same pattern.

2

The Gipper

At the age of seventeen, Dutch, along with his sweetheart Margaret Cleaver, enrolled in Eureka College, a small teaching college south of Dixon run by the Disciples of Christ. He couldn't afford even the modest tuition, so he negotiated his way into the freshman class by offering to pay off the three-hundred-dollar-a-year fee by washing dishes, coaching sports teams, and swimming competitively.

It didn't take Reagan long to plunge into campus life wholeheartedly, joining a student strike against proposed cutbacks in the faculty and curriculum and the possibility that the whole school might move wholesale to a place where more Disciples lived to support it. It was there—during that strike—that Reagan first found his public voice. In a speech denouncing Bert Wilson, the school president, as "morally evil," he brought the student body to its feet, according to *Ronnie and Nancy*. Colacello quotes Howard Short, one of the strike's organizers as saying that Dutch had "the biggest mouth of the freshman class. . . . He was a cocky SOB, a loud talker. Dutch was the guy you wanted to put up there."

Wilson resigned, and for the first time Ronald Reagan glimpsed the power of a public platform, sensed the heady feeling that comes when your words have the power to change people and events. Still, he channeled most of his energies in Eureka not into politics but into football. His grades were just good enough for him to stay eligible for extracurricular activities—football primarily, but also the drama club. He made the football team but then spent the first year on the bench.

It was still a grim time for the family. The Depression hit home, the store closed, and then Jack, reduced to working as a traveling salesman, lost his job over Christmas. Nelle made ends meet as a saleswoman and seamstress. Reagan, who was earning money as a swimming coach, sent his mother cash from time to time to buy food.

Reagan graduated college in the heart of the Great Depression. He didn't have a distinguished academic record, but he did earn a reputation as a football player and as an actor in school plays. He also had his mentors. Powerful men and women would spot him, see something they sometimes could put into words, sometimes not, and want to put their credibility, their goodwill, and later their fortunes, on the line in the service of helping Ronald Reagan achieve whatever awaited him. One had been Walgreen. Another was Sid Altschuler, a Kansas City businessman married to a Dixon girl. Altschuler and his family spent their summers in Dixon, and Reagan taught his daughters to swim. The two met, and Altschuler, like so many, looked at the strapping young lifeguard with the amiable demeanor and glimpsed the promise of . . . something.

When he asked Reagan what he really wanted to do in life, Ron told him he wanted to be a radio sportscaster. (By now Reagan really wanted to be an actor, but wasn't ready to voice his ambition—people in Dixon didn't become Hollywood stars, or even think about it.)

"If that's what you want," Altschuler said, "then go ahead and do it. Only go at it wholeheartedly. Give it all you've got."

Caught up with the romance and glamour of the new medium, Reagan took the advice to heart. He hitchhiked to Chicago, intending to break in with one of the big radio networks. Becoming increasingly disheartened, he trudged from one to another, getting nowhere. This being radio, his good looks were of no advantage. Eventually, at one station, he ran into a receptionist who took pity on him and advised him that starting at the top wasn't an option; there was too much competition, and he didn't have the credentials. Go back to the sticks, young man, she said, go get some experience.

That's exactly what he did, starting with a five-dollar bus ride to a University of Iowa football game and an eventual broadcasting job in Davenport, Iowa, where he worked for B. J. Palmer, one of the great entrepreneurial oddballs of the time. Palmer owned the radio station, plus an eclectic cluster of other businesses, including something called Little Bit o' Heaven (a so-called garden of wonders), a printing press, a dance hall, a roller rink, restaurants—and the Palmer School of Chiropractic, run mainly by family members. Palmer was, in fact, the son of Daniel David Palmer, who, believing that all ailments could be traced to spinal misalignment, created chiropractic in the late nineteenth century. (B. J. was also accused of contributing to his father's death in 1913 by deliberately running over him with his car during a parade, but that's probably not true.) The broadcasting studio, where Reagan learned his craft as an announcer, was on the top floor of the building that housed the chiropractic school, which was, in turn, next door to another Palmer enterprise, described as "the heavenly Buddhist shrine." Quiet little Davenport contained more than enough strangeness to lay a foundation to prepare him for Hollywood.

From Davenport, Reagan moved onward and upward to become chief sports announcer for WHO, the Palmer-owned NBC affiliate in Des Moines, Iowa. He lived frugally and apportioned his money carefully—some to his mother, some to his brother, some set aside to marry Margaret, to whom he had become engaged.

But then Margaret changed her mind. After graduation, she taught for a year and joined her sister in Paris, where, as people will do when they go to Paris, she fell in love, in her case with a foreign service officer. She sent back Dutch's fraternity pin and engagement ring.

"Our lovely and wholesome relationship did not survive growing up," he later reflected.

He wasn't lonely for long, however. Dutch was a big, handsome young man—even some of the women among the seventy-seven (or seventy-eight) near-drowning victims in the Rock River, it was suggested, might have been immobilized by a cramp that started in the heartstrings, one that would put them into the capable arms of the lifeguard with the movie-star looks. Reagan always denied that, but his son Ronald Jr. in *My Father's Memories* does quote one Dixon beauty saying years later, "I had a friend who nearly drowned herself trying to get him to save her." No matter, though. How she got into the difficulty isn't the point; it's who rescued her.

Of course, his appeal to women didn't escape Reagan's notice. He spent five exciting years in Des Moines, becoming a local celebrity, invited to dinners, invited to speak at clubs, able to meet a lot of young women while he developed a small but steady reputation across the Midwest as a sports announcer.

Reagan mastered the trick of reading the wire service play-by-play, brought to him by an assistant named Curly, of major league baseball games and re-creating the action on the air for his listeners—even though he had never actually seen a major league game. It was a common enough technique for sportscasters who couldn't get to the actual games, and it gave him a flair for imagining events beyond the horizon. It also honed his skill at ad-libbing. When he told Nancy, with a bullet in him after a 1981 assassination attempt, "Honey, I forgot to duck!" (quoting Jack Dempsey after his defeat by Gene Tunney in 1926), he was calling on those skills.

In his autobiography, Reagan recalled his greatest moment as a quick-thinking broadcaster. He was announcing a Chicago Cubs baseball game that was already in the ninth inning when Curly handed him a note that read: "The wire has gone dead."

"I had a ball on the way to the plate and no way to call it back," he wrote. "At the same time, I was convinced that a ball game tied up in the ninth inning was no time to tell my audience we had lost contact with the game and they would have to listen to recorded music. I knew of only one thing that wouldn't get in the score column and betray me—a foul ball."

As he desperately waited for the wire service to regain contact with the game, Reagan kept describing the batter hitting foul ball after foul ball off pitch after pitch. In between describing the pitches, he even told his audience about a red-haired kid who kept running up in the stands to retrieve the foul balls.

"My voice was rising in pitch and threatening to crack—and then, bless him, Curly started typing. I clutched at the slip. It said: 'Galan popped out on the first ball pitched.' Not in my game he didn't—he popped out after practically making a career of foul balls."

Reagan was in his early twenties and filled with the optimism instilled by Nelle and the Disciples of Christ. And he knew he was good-looking. By 1937, aged twenty-six, he was ready for Hollywood. He wanted to act. Other radio guys had made the transition, and he felt he could too.

He landed an assignment on the West Coast covering the Cubs training camp on Catalina Island, and used his spare time to meet with a Hollywood agent. The agent set up a screen test, and Reagan was on his way. No more radio. No more fictionalized baseball play-by-play. And no more Midwest. In 1937, Warner Bros. signed him to a six-month contract—and promptly cast him as a radio announcer in his first real part, in *Love Is in the Air*. He appeared in eight movies that first year.

His career didn't skyrocket, but there was always steady work. Reagan's solid, reliable, familiar face radiated with all of the sturdy values embedded in the American heartland. All of his roles seemed to cast him as more or less himself: a good-looking farm boy with all-American looks and an "aw-shucks" attitude. He always played the good sport, losing the girl, letting the star walk away with the big scenes, accepting the smaller credit.

But after all those unsettled years in Illinois, moving from river town to river town in his childhood, he had finally found a home. Hollywood suited him. He had a lucrative career and he had a circle of friends. As a handsome, eligible bachelor with a likeable personality, he was a welcome dinner guest at Jack Benny's home, Robert Taylor's home. He socialized with Bogart and Bacall, Robert Stack, Burns and Allen, Pat O'Brien, James Cagney, Dick Powell and June Allyson, George Murphy. He called them friends, and they all seemed to take him under their wings.

He dated beautiful women, including Doris Day, Piper Laurie, and Rhonda Fleming. With his newfound income, he bought his parents a house in West Hollywood—the first they had ever owned—and helped his brother, Neil, get a job as a staff announcer for WFWB, the Warner Bros. radio station.

Nelle did what she always did: She joined a local Disciples of Christ church, while keeping close ties to the one back home in Dixon. Jack, too, had a few good years, before dying in 1941.

Life had taken a sweet seismic shift for Reagan. If he wasn't exactly Errol Flynn—he jokingly referred to himself as "the Errol Flynn of B-movies"—he was still having a fine season and making almost as much money as Flynn.

He shone in *Brother Rat* in 1938, trying to convince the studios that he had real acting chops. But the verdict on Reagan was that he was hopelessly nice—too nice to be the leading man and definitely too nice to be the villain.

The studio moguls viewed him with a kind of tolerant condescension—even after his most dramatic performance in *Knute Rockne, All American* (1940), in which he played the tragic halfback George Gipp. On his deathbed, the movie version of Gipp utters one of Reagan's two immortal movie lines: "Win one for the Gipper." It became a battle cry in his later life.

The second enduring line came from *King's Row*, in 1942, in which Reagan plays Drake, a heedless playboy who wakes up after an accident to find his legs have been amputated by a doctor angry that Drake has seduced his daughter. He delivers the cry that became the title of his autobiography: "Where's the rest of me?"

Why he never became a top-flight star is hard to explain, but it has to do with how he projected on screen, and in real life. Reagan was likeable—even loveable—but there was an odd detachment about him, as if his attention were somewhere else, someplace far away. It was, if anybody had the wisdom to spot it, the unknowable mystery that lies at the heart of leadership. Doris Day, his costar in *Storm Warning*, described a date with the hunky Reagan: "When he wasn't dancing he was talking. It wasn't really a conversation, it was rather like talking at you, sort of long discourses on subjects that interested him. I remember telling him that he should be touring the country making speeches." She turned out to be prescient.

In 1938, a year after his arrival in Hollywood, when he was making *Brother Rat*, Reagan fell in love with costar Jane Wyman. She was married at the time, and it took until 1940 before she and Reagan were able to tie the knot. They were an ideal couple, and they had an ideal marriage; that's the way Ronnie and Jane were pitched to the fan magazines in the early '40s. They had adorable children—Maureen, born in 1941, and Michael, adopted in 1946. (Tragically, Christine, born prematurely in 1947, died within twenty-four hours of her birth.) The family photographs were all over the media. Smiling, happy, ideal.

By 1940, Reagan's career was just gaining traction—starring with Flynn in *Santa Fe Trail*—and his salary had tripled. Then World War II came. Reagan reported for duty in 1942, and discovered that his eyesight wasn't good enough for him to serve in anything approaching a combat outfit. As told in Peter Schweizer's *Reagan's War*, the conversation went like this:

> *"If we sent you overseas, you'd shoot a general," one doctor told him.*
> *"Yes," said the other. "And you'd miss him."*

Reagan, however, received a commission and was assigned to the Army Air Corps Motion Picture Unit in Culver City producing training films. He also appeared in the Irving Berlin movie *This Is the Army*. By the time he was discharged, he was a captain.

The three-year interruption slowed his career, and his next important roles were "mature" roles—in the likes of *That Hagen Girl* and *The Girl from Jones Beach*—parts for an actor past the prime of a matinee idol. He was so likeable as the best friend that Reagan simply wasn't offered any of the meatier roles after the war. *King's Row* and *Knute Rockne* were dismissed as anomalies, moments of the past. In the end, the studios decided that he wasn't weighty enough, that he didn't contain the interior fire of a Flynn or a Clark Gable.

It was also after the war that Reagan's marriage began to fall apart. Some rumors had it that Jane had fallen in love with Lew Ayers, her *Johnny Belinda* costar. Others said she had never recovered from the loss of Christine in 1947. Still others blamed the 1948 Academy Award she received for her performance as a deaf-mute rape victim in *Johnny Belinda* (the first Oscar of the sound era for a non-speaking part), citing envy on Reagan's part as a motive for the breakup. But anyone who knew Reagan wouldn't credit him with behavior that petty. And he seemed genuinely stunned by the divorce. "It was, you know, just terrible because he was very unhappy," the actress Patricia Neal said in an interview years later. "He was in an apartment by himself. . . . He was heartbroken. He really was, because he didn't want a divorce from her. But Jane wanted it."

Eventually, Reagan absorbed the shock of divorce as he did almost all the blows in his life: with grace and good cheer. Wyman forever spoke glowingly of him. Above all, they were both concerned for the children.

Back in 1940, when they were newlyweds, Ron and Jane had joined the Screen Actors Guild. The next year, he attended his first meeting of the board of directors as an alternate vote. He began to assert himself, speaking out on issues that affected the industry—and he had no shortage of opinions. SAG became, in a real way, an introduction to politics for Reagan.

At SAG, Reagan became a critic of other unions that were more left-wing; he was a liberal anti-Communist. When unions in the film industry went on strike during the war, he attacked them as unpatriotic. Once the war was over, he quickly realized that there was another menace threatening America: Communism. It wasn't just the Communists in Moscow; homegrown Communists were infiltrating American institutions, too. Hollywood, with its potential for influencing American minds, was a particular target.

By 1947, SAG was in turmoil because of a technicality in the conflict-of-interest clause in the new bylaws. Board members James Cagney, John Garfield, Harpo Marx, Dennis O'Keefe, Dick Powell, and Franchot Tone all resigned.

At the March 10 meeting, Reagan showed up late—and arrived to find he had been elected president of SAG. He presided so sensibly over stormy sessions and held reasonable ground when issues of free speech and congressional interference rose up that SAG elected him president seven times. He also fought a courageous and principled battle against the encroaching Communists.

He had already notched one significant victory over the Reds when he was serving on the executive committee of a group called the Hollywood Independent Citizens Committee of Arts, Sciences and Professions (HICCASP), which he had joined in 1944. The membership ranged from Albert Einstein to Frank Sinatra—about as wide a range as you could hope to find anywhere. It fretted about atomic weapons, warned about the resurgence of fascism, and expressed concern about the Cold War. It also seemed to support the Soviet line whenever the subject came up. "My first evangelism," he said later, "came in the form of being hell-bent on saving the world from neofascism."

But HICCASP also aroused the suspicions of the FBI. According to Arthur Schlesinger Jr., writing in *Life* magazine, it was a Communist front organization where "celebrities maintained their membership but not their vigilance." Surprised and appalled, a small anti-Communist group inside HICCASP decided to see if Schlesinger's accusation was true. Here's what happened at the board of directors' meeting, as told by Seth Rosenfeld in 2012's *Subversives: The FBI's War on Student Radicals, and Reagan's Rise to Power:*

> *A heated debate quickly erupted when James Roosevelt, FDR's son, took the floor and declared that organizations like HICCASP must be "vigilant against being used by Communist sympathizers."* . . . *Other board members harshly criticized Roosevelt's proposal. Reagan was disturbed by this and mentioned it to Dore Schary, the head of MGM, who was sitting beside him. As the meeting broke up, Schary invited Reagan to stop by the home of the actress Olivia de Havilland, a board member who had starred in* Gone with the Wind.

Reagan raced over to de Havilland's apartment, to find a gathering of concerned HICCASP board members. "I was amazed when she and others in the room said they suspected Communists were trying to take over the organization," Reagan wrote in An American Life. *"As we talked over the situation, I turned to her and whispered: 'You know, Olivia, I always thought* you *might be one of 'them.'" She laughed and said, 'That's funny. I thought* you *were one of them.'"*

Reagan had planned only to listen during this meeting, given that he was a new board member. "But. . . I suggested that we propose a resolution to the executive committee with language that we knew a Communist couldn't accept and have Olivia submit it in the next meeting the following week and see what happened," he wrote. Reagan drafted the motion, which declared, "We reaffirm belief in free enterprise and the democratic system and repudiate Communism as desirable for the United States."

When the July 2, 1946, meeting came around, Roosevelt noted that HICCASP had many times denounced fascism, which it had. For the sake of consistency in defense of democratic values, it should also denounce Communism, the other totalitarian enemy. He offered his support for the resolution—and the meeting exploded into what Reagan would later call "a Kilkenny brawl."

Bandleader Artie Shaw offered to recite the Soviet constitution from memory—as if the guarantees in the Soviet constitution meant anything at the time of Stalin's gulags. Screenwriter Dalton Trumbo denounced the anti-Soviet resolution. Another screenwriter and veteran Communist, John Howard Lawson, waved his finger in Reagan's face and told him to watch it. Reagan was called, among other things, a fascist, "capitalist scum," "witch-hunter," "red-baiter," and "enemy of the proletariat."

The HICCASP's executive board, with the stalwart exception of Olivia de Havilland, voted down the resolution. That was it for Reagan; he, de Havilland, James Roosevelt, and the other anti-Communists immediately resigned from the organization. It collapsed shortly thereafter.

But the day before, another, bigger issue exploded. The left-wing Conference of Studio Unions, embroiled in an ongoing jurisdictional battle with the International Alliance of Theatrical Stage Employees (IATSE) called a strike. It was settled quickly thanks to the intervention of an emergency SAG committee. Reagan was one of the committee members, and soon he became an indispensable fighter in the ongoing battle over Communism in the unions.

The peace agreement—it was dubbed the Treaty of Beverly Hills—fell apart quickly, and the two craft unions were soon at each other's throats again. The CSU engaged muscle from the longshoremen's union; IATSE called on its allies in the Teamsters union. It got very ugly very quickly. Reagan, who along with other stars was ignoring the CSU's picket lines, started getting midnight phone calls. He was working on a movie called *Night after Night* at the time. "There's a group being formed to deal with you," he was told. "They're going to fix you so you won't ever act again." Fearing that CSU thugs were planning to throw acid in his face—which had happened to one studio employee already—the studio issued him a .32 Smith & Wesson. He hired guards to watch his kids. "I have been looking over my shoulder when I go down the street," he told a SAG meeting.

One tactic the studio developed to protect its workers, including actors working on movies, was to sneak them in through a storm drain. Reagan preferred to go in with all flags flying and all drums beating. He began riding a bus that passed through the rock- and bottle-throwing CSU pickets. One of the buses was destroyed by a firebomb, but still he persisted.

After the strike began, SAG voted to cross the picket line. But there were CSU supporters among SAG's leadership, and they suggested that the Guild try to arbitrate some kind of solution. Reagan, by now, however, had had enough of the CSU and their type. And, eventually, he brought the membership of SAG along with him; the actors voted ten-to-one to keep working. It was the end of the CSU. Without the actors, they didn't have a chance.

He had found a training ground for higher office. And years later, when he was in the White House, he would draw parallels between his battles against Communists in Hollywood and the ones who ruled in the Kremlin. "I know it sounds kind of foolish to link Hollywood, and experience there, to the world situation," he said in 1981, "and yet, the tactics seemed to be pretty much the same."

Reagan was, like James Roosevelt, a Democrat and a liberal.

If you want a surreal experience, check out the YouTube video of Reagan from 1948, lambasting the Republicans in Congress and the big corporations whose excessive profits, he said, were driving prices through the roof to the detriment of working-class America. Then he goes on to say: "This is why we must have new faces in the Congress of the United States.

"Democratic faces.

"This is why we must elect not only President Truman, but also men like Mayor Hubert Humphrey of Minneapolis, the Democratic candidate for senator from Minnesota."

Harry Truman?

Hubert Humphrey?

Ronald Reagan?

Those endorsements made for the high-water mark of Reagan's liberal phase. From then on, the tide began to ebb slowly but appreciably, until by 1964 he was throwing the full weight of his eloquence into the lost cause of Barry Goldwater's run for the White House. The

Goldwater ticket would be beaten badly by Lyndon Johnson and his running mate—the same Hubert Humphrey who Reagan endorsed so cheerfully in 1948.

His career, meanwhile, staggered along.

Always a realist, Reagan saw the writing on the wall. In 1947, he was cast opposite Shirley Temple in *That Hagen Girl*, a lighter-than-air comedy. The script's whiff of romance between a seventeen-year-old girl and a thirty-six-year-old man embarrassed him. But, as always, he was a good sport about it. He played the part with his usual sincerity—he had the chops—but it had become clear that he wasn't ever going to be a leading man. As if that weren't bad enough, *The Girl from Jones Beach* in 1949 and his signature performance in a role of pure fluff, 1951's *Bedtime for Bonzo*, in which he played opposite a chimp, confirmed his standing. He was cast, as usual, as a college professor—an unthreatening male presence somewhere between a father and an uncle.

Despite *The Hasty Heart*, a rare dramatic turn, the parts were empty froth that almost insulted his dignity, the likes of *John Loves Mary* and *She's Working Her Way through College*. He felt himself on the cusp of being cast as a buffoon.

He did, however, meet a young actress named Nancy Davis. Here's how she describes it in her 2000 book *I Love You, Ronnie: The Letters of Ronald Reagan to Nancy Reagan:*

> *We'd met in the fall of 1950 on a blind date—that is to say a date that was blind for Ronnie but not for me. I'd seen him in pictures—and I liked what I saw. I was doing a picture—*East Side, West Side—*for Mervyn LeRoy, an old family friend, at Metro, when I saw my name on a list of Communist sympathizers. I went to Mervyn and said I was upset and asked if there was anything he could do. Later, it turned out that it was another Nancy Davis, but I was upset, so I said to Mervyn, "It's not right. You've got to do something."*

Mervyn said not to worry; he would have the studio plant an item in Louella Parsons' column. The next day I went to him again and said, "A little item in Louella Parsons isn't enough. My family's really upset." So Mervyn said, "I'll call Ronald Reagan. He's president of the Screen Actors Guild, and he'll be able to straighten things out. Come to think of it," he went on, "I think you two should know each other."

Now that seemed like a very good idea.

"Yes, Mervyn," I said, remembering the handsome man I'd seen in movies, "I think so, too."

"I'll call him," he said. "And he'll call you."

But Ronnie didn't call, so the next day on the set, I said, "Mervyn, I'm really worried about this."

So Mervyn called Ronnie again.

Ronnie told me later that he couldn't understand why Mervyn was making such a fuss, but he called me that same day and asked me to go to dinner. "It'll have to be early, though," he said. "I have an early call."

I said, "Yes, I have an early call, too." I didn't—and he didn't—but we wanted to protect ourselves. He didn't even know what I looked like.

Ronnie was on crutches that night, having recently broken his leg in a charity baseball game.

"How come you moved in on me like this?" Ronnie would write to me from a lonely hotel room years later, when he was away on one of his long trips for GE. Why do people fall in love? It's almost impossible to say. If you're not a teenager or in your early twenties, you've gone on a lot of dates and met a lot of people. When the real thing comes along, you just know it, at least I did.

So did Ron. Nancy was to be the love of his life.

Nancy's stepfather, neurosurgeon Loyal Davis, who was a staunchly conservative Republican who lived in Arizona and was friends with Barry Goldwater, would have a great influence on Reagan's political convictions, as would Nancy. How conservative was Loyal Davis? When his reliably Republican hometown, Galesburg, Illinois, voted for Johnson over Goldwater in 1964, he grumpily announced that he no longer wished to be buried there.

At the same time, Reagan shifted his sagging career to the small screen. By 1954, with a second family to support—he and Nancy now had Patti and Ron Jr.—Reagan took on the role of TV host of *General Electric Theater*. It was an unlikely springboard, but was the first step to greater things. The next step, according to Lou Cannon's *Governor Reagan*, seemed like a random event: Reagan was asked to make a speech on behalf of the United Fund at a GE plant. A GE public relations man who was there told Reagan that he'd been rejecting requests for speeches because he hated writing them. Reagan told him not to worry, he didn't need a speechwriter. "If you want to accept a speaking date for me, I'll take care of it," he said.

"Once GE found that Reagan could speak," Cannon's book relates, "the company wouldn't let him stop. By Reagan's account, he gave as many as fourteen speeches a day and spent a total of two years of the eight he was under contract to General Electric on the road, visiting every one of the company's plants and meeting all of its 250,000 employees."

Responding to questions from corporate audiences concerned with government waste, he began to address the issue, in the process becoming more critical of Big Government. His talks were designed to raise the workers' morale while having the added advantage of boosting the company's image. Almost by accident, he created a national constituency—a public that would remember when it came time to show its support.

Reagan was the ideal man for the job. His avuncular style seemed to validate his authority. And he began to change. The New Deal Reagan began to disappear; the conservative Reagan began to take shape.

He was angry, and he spoke passionately against big government. But in 1959, he denounced the Tennessee Valley Authority, beloved by Roosevelt Democrats as a symbol of the power of government to do good. That, however, wasn't what got Reagan in trouble with his corporate bosses. The problem was that the TVA did $50 million a year in business with GE. He had, inadvertently, bitten the hand that fed him.

At first, GE, in the person of its CEO and chairman, Ralph Cordiner, defended him. He was within his rights, they told him; he did not need to bend to corporate pressure. But the reality was different; his days were numbered, and in 1962, the company cut him loose. He was adrift professionally, if not personally. He had Nancy and the children to support.

It was, in a real sense, only the beginning.

3

The Speech

I had never heard it before, the speech everyone was talking about. It was the speech that Reagan delivered for Barry Goldwater right before the 1964 presidential campaign. It didn't help Goldwater, whom Lyndon Johnson crushed, but it catapulted Reagan into the political limelight. That was about the only thing that people talked about after that huge Republican defeat—or at least all the conservatives talked about.

In 1964—less than a year after President Kennedy had been assassinated, the whole political world still emotionally fragile—the Republican Convention took place at the Cow Palace in San Francisco where Barry Goldwater was nominated to run against incumbent Democrat Lyndon Johnson. While there was very little chance that Goldwater could win, he captured the heart of the Republican Party with his square jaw and refusal to budge on issues. Nonetheless, important Republicans already were looking ahead for someone who could appeal to a broad range of Americans, including blue-collar Democrats, someone who could actually win the presidency. Ronald Reagan caught their eye.

By now, as he wrote in *An American Life,* Reagan had had the epiphany that caused him to part company, once and for all, from the Democratic Party to which he had once been so loyal.

"One day I came home and said to Nancy, 'You know, something just dawned on me. All those things I've been saying about government in my speeches (I wasn't just making speeches, I was preaching a sermon), all these things I've been criticizing about government being too big, well, it just dawned on me that every four years when an election comes along, I go out and support the people who are responsible for the things I've been criticizing.'"

Then, he said, "I remained a Democrat for another two years, but by 1960, I'd completed the process of self-conversion."

So in the doomed year of 1964, the backers decided to give Reagan a kind of minor-league tryout and, at the same time, make a last-ditch attempt to win it for Goldwater. Republican backers bought network airtime and allowed Ronald Reagan to deliver The Speech, which you can read, in its entirety, in the appendix to this book.

Reagan had given that same speech, more or less, hundreds of times in hundreds of GE plants to thousands of employees. The speech—The Speech—helped give birth to his first group of organized supporters—the Friends of Ronald Reagan. They were politicians, businessmen, and show-business pals. It was a cast of characters that would change and grow as his career grew and more and more people saw the possibilities.

As The Speech reverberated, they all reacted to the sharp clarity of Reagan's call to arms. They wanted him to run for the US Senate, like George Murphy, or run for governor of California. He wasn't exactly an amateur when it came to public speaking, so that TV ad he did for Goldwater on the eve of the '64 election expanded the stage.

As I said, I had never heard the speech delivered in person, although I had a pretty good idea of what was in it. When a poster announcing that Ronald Reagan was going to appear locally and talk politics crossed my path, I made it my business to show up.

This was in October of '65, three months before he officially declared for governor. He was appearing in a small classroom at the Brentwood Elementary School, about twenty minutes from my home. A small group of like-minded conservatives, we all squeezed into antiquated wooden kids' chairs.

Even in that tiny, remote classroom, Reagan came as a surprise. He wore a finely tailored sports jacket and immaculately pressed slacks. I don't know how far he had traveled, but his shirt was crisp, his tie knotted perfectly. He had a warm smile and seemed to acknowledge everyone in the room. There were just seventeen of us there, mostly couples, and even for that small number he turned it on.

He was, after all, a movie star.

He stood in front of the blackboard, the room decorated with children's drawings so that it felt . . . well, it felt as if we were going to receive a lesson. I was transfixed.

Sitting in a chair looking up at him adoringly was Nancy, her face aglow; she watched her husband's every move, hung on his every word. She couldn't take her eyes off him, and I couldn't take my eyes off the two of them. Her presence offered a kind of affirming testimony. It was something to see.

The speech, "A Time for Choosing," laid out a common-sense case for conservatism, making a thrilling declaration of ideological independence and ringing with noble courage. Essentially, it was a rational man's attack on big government.

Do I remember every word he said? After almost half a century? Of course not. I have to reread it for the exact words. But I remember exactly how I felt, the thrill, the sense of the hairs standing up on the back of my neck, and, yes, tears welling in my eyes at several crucial moments. And the version of the speech I heard that night was the same version, with tweaks, he had been delivering for years. The feeling I have today is like the feeling you have years after the first time you sit through a performance of Beethoven's *Fifth Symphony*. You don't remember the notes that were played, or how; you just remember the emotions it drew from you. So, here goes:

Reagan would have started out addressing our economic situation:

"We haven't balanced our budget twenty-eight out of the last thirty-four years," he told us. "We've raised our debt limit three times in the last twelve months, and now our national debt is one and a half times bigger than all the combined debts of all the nations of the world. We have fifteen billion dollars in gold in our treasury; we don't own an ounce. Foreign dollar claims are 27.3 billion dollars. And we've just had announced that the dollar of 1939 will now purchase forty-five cents in its total value."

So far, so good. Good, common-sense fiscal conservatism. Nothing that we hadn't heard from other politicians over the years.

But that wasn't Reagan's theme. His real cause was freedom, how fragile it is, and how it needs to be fought for, generation after generation. Two decades before the enemy had been in Berlin and Tokyo. Now he resided in Moscow and Peking—and closer to home. Reagan took on the peaceniks and the neo-isolationists of the Left. "As for the peace that we would preserve," he said, "I wonder who among us would like to approach the wife or mother whose husband or son has died in South Vietnam and ask them if they think this is a peace that should be maintained indefinitely.

"Do they mean peace, or do they mean we just want to be left in peace? There can be no real peace while one American is dying some place in the world for the rest of us."

Maybe a tear or two, at this moment, thinking of my friend George Jones dying at Pearl Harbor, and the boys who had died in Korea, and the ones who were in harm's way in Vietnam. Different enemies, but always for that same cause of freedom.

34

"We're at war with the most dangerous enemy that has ever faced mankind in his long climb from the swamp to the stars, and it's been said if we lose that war, and in so doing lose this way of freedom of ours, history will record with the greatest astonishment that those who had the most to lose did the least to prevent its happening. Well I think it's time we ask ourselves if we still know the freedoms that were intended for us by the Founding Fathers."

Reagan told a favorite story, not for the first time, and not for the last:

"Not too long ago, two friends of mine were talking to a Cuban refugee, a businessman who had escaped from Castro, and in the midst of his story one of my friends turned to the other and said, 'We don't know how lucky we are.' And the Cuban stopped and said, 'How lucky you are? I had someplace to escape to.' And in that sentence he told us the entire story. If we lose freedom here, there's no place to escape to. This is the last stand on earth."

I remembered that story decades later in 2000 when the government of the time returned young Elián González to Cuba after he had escaped from that ramshackle hellhole—and his mother drowned in the attempt. At the time, I thought: He had someplace to escape to, and we sent him back. Maybe after Castro and his cronies are finally gone, Elián will be able to come here again and tell people how he really felt about being sent back. I know Ronald Reagan wouldn't have sent him back.

It made a lot of sense and contained some thrilling head-slappers. Here's Reagan's take on foreign aid. He wasn't against it as such, but it had, since the end of World War II, gotten way out of hand—and there were too many hands, grubby, bloodstained, unworthy hands, reaching out for it.

"I think," he said, "we're for aiding our allies by sharing of our material blessings with those nations which share in our fundamental beliefs, but we're against doling out money government to government, creating bureaucracy, if not socialism, all over the world. We set out to help nineteen countries. We're helping 107. We've spent 146 billion dollars. With that money, we bought a 2-million-dollar yacht for Haile Selassie [Ethiopia's medieval emperor]. We bought dress suits for Greek undertakers, extra wives for Kenyan government officials. We bought a thousand TV sets for a place where they have no electricity. In the last six years, fifty-two nations have bought seven billion dollars' worth of our gold, and all fifty-two are receiving foreign aid from this country."

He also attacked Social Security, not the program itself, but the inefficiency and deficits that went with it (and that have only grown in the years since). He pointed out that a private investment returned $220 a month as opposed to the $127 the government was paying out to seniors then. He attacked bureaucracy; he lambasted government waste. He proclaimed freedom and the wisdom of the Founding Fathers.

But here was the part that brought the tears to my eyes again:

"You and I are told increasingly we have to choose between a Left or Right. Well I'd like to suggest there is no such thing as a Left or Right. There's only an up or down—[up is] man's old dream, the ultimate in individual freedom consistent with law and order, or down to the ant heap of totalitarianism. And regardless of their sincerity, their humanitarian motives, those who would trade our freedom for security have embarked on this downward course."

Now he was saying things no one else was saying, and he was saying them with an eloquence that moved the soul. It was all music to the ears of a beleaguered Republican. He was speaking to me. He spoke of how hard it was to go against the prevailing winds, and that, too, struck home. (It's no picnic being a Republican on a liberal Democrat campus.)

This was a man who'd been tested. He'd endured a few trials of his own.

Reagan started out as a New Deal Democrat, but he ran into trouble when his beliefs began to shift, when he started to doubt the wisdom of surrendering his rights, when he resisted efforts by the Left to take over his union.

He told us how they had gone after him during the Hollywood labor wars of the 1940s, how they threatened to throw acid in his face. Even if it was an empty threat, it was particularly nasty—like threatening to break the fingers of a concert pianist. He told us how he wouldn't even dare open his front door without first making sure that no one was waiting outside to disfigure him.

That's when I saw, up close, his integrity. This wasn't a man who easily backed down in the face of violent threats. I believe that I saw that night what a lot of people came to recognize as his brave streak of uncompromising purpose, the bold certainty that came from the heart of that teacher who stood at the head of the classroom. I saw a glimmer of it in that little classroom.

But at the end, I have to say, his appearance there that night also struck me as a little sad. This must, I thought at the time, be a very low point for him—appearing at a half-empty classroom in an out-of-the-way section of the state. Of course, soon I began to appreciate that this was tactical, something like an out-of-town tryout. He was just clearing his throat for the bigger platform. But I didn't know that when I went to the school. I was just an innocent bystander, drawn to the talk by sheer curiosity. At the time I was an assistant professor of behavioral psychology—a lonely Republican in the desert of the Democrat-dominated world of academia.

When the talk ended, people approached him. We were all a little shy, I suppose, a little embarrassed that such a big, important man had to appear in such a small setting. I worked up the nerve to ask him if he ever thought of running for political office.

He looked at Nancy, and they exchanged knowing smiles, so I knew that this wasn't something out of the blue. Clearly he'd been asked before. But he ducked the question and said something vague, like, "It's never come up . . ."

4

Behavior Modification

I was, at the time, in late 1965, an assistant professor in clinical psychology at San Fernando Valley State College. I had escaped to there after a miserable year teaching postgraduate students at the Neuropsychiatric Institute (NPI) at UCLA. The mission of the NPI, an accredited part of the UCLA medical complex, was to train doctors in the psychiatric arts as well as to provide patient care. In other words, our chief job was to turn doctors into psychiatrists.

But there was also the research, a big part of the NPI's task. The culture of America was undergoing a vast transformation in the 1960s, and it was not clearly understood. What, for example, provoked and sustained urban unrest? What were the roots of the emerging so-called counterculture? Why were young people whose fathers and uncles had stormed beaches in Normandy and the Pacific in their names suddenly turning against all that had been accepted in America—democracy, decency, even personal hygiene. Questions needed to be asked, answers had to be found.

Until 1961, the NPI had been woven into the medical system of the university, with classrooms scattered all over the campus—no central command center. There were a few score beds for inpatient psychiatric care in the hospital, but the treatment was diffuse and difficult to monitor. The decision to consolidate the NPI into one specific area of the medical complex meant dislocation and a kind of artless improvisation. Until a main unit was in place, new buildings went up quickly, mostly made of wood. My first office had no desk, but it did have a Bunsen burner, which has no known use in psychiatry; I suppose I could have used it to make coffee, if I drank coffee.

I was teaching abnormal psychology in large lecture halls with 150 graduate students—not the way that I was taught psychology at Ohio State. And the budding psychiatrists were assigned a full caseload of patients from the get-go even though many of them had had only one or two psychology classes during their undergraduate years or in medical school. The program was slapped together in a hurry and without comprehensive or systematic order. In fact, to get unpaid assistance for classroom demonstrations of psychiatric techniques, civilian volunteers were actually plucked off the street. If they were troubled when they came in to pose as patients, they were probably in worse shape when they'd been worked over by our rookie psychiatrists. It was no way to train psychiatrists.

But apart from the poor planning and all-encompassing chaos that comes with such a bumpy startup, the whole atmosphere on the campus was uncomfortable for me. I was, very quickly, unhappy with the tone of UCLA. It was a very liberal campus, so my political beliefs put me completely out of place.

I wasn't totally alone.

Dr. Stanley Plog, who became an eminent clinical psychologist, not to mention my business partner and lifelong friend, was another atypical member of the staff. He also fell into the fatal category of cultural misfit.

What was it that put us at such odds with our colleagues? We were—horror of horrors!—conservative Republicans. Even worse, we looked like conservative Republicans, and, shamelessly so, living in the

Stan (right) and I in 1968 at Lockheed's legendary "Skunk Works" location, a smaller hangar tucked away in the Burbank airport, where we were working with their international marketing division. Clarence "Kelly" Johnson, the famous engineer who masterminded the P-38, the U-2, and finally the SR-71, was sitting several tables away in the executive dining room. Stan, who didn't have many street smarts, asked the person next to him in a fairly loud voice, "Are you still building the U-2?" The whole room froze into absolute silence. Nobody knew what to say. After five or ten seconds, I said, "Stan, I guess you got your answer!"

belly of the university's shaggy-haired, woolly-minded liberal beast. To the overwhelming majority of the UCLA population—both students and faculty—our crew cuts, sports jackets, clean shirts, proper neckties, and pressed khakis might as well have been war paint. We were wearing the uniform of their enemies, and we didn't care.

Stan and I met at UCLA in 1960 when he was thirty and I was thirty-three. He was still an intern at the time. I had my doctorate, but even then I was growing more and more disaffected from the environment. Our meeting was one of those happy flukes.

One day I saw this guy walking across campus lugging a big box loaded with IBM computer punch cards—the first kind of information storage devices, originally developed by the French textile industry and the first precursors to floppy disks, data CDs, and data stored in the Cloud. The cards, the way he carried himself, the cut of his hair—and it was cut very short—these were all important recognition symbols. (The musical *Hair*, approaching the issue from the opposite viewpoint, recognized the importance of the symbolism.) The computer cards told me that he was a serious person involved in some kind of high-tech research. Who else but a devoted nerd—I don't think the word had even been coined yet—would lug around all of those computer printout cards? But even more significant, I had an instinctive feeling that he was someone sympathetic. No sideburns, no elbow patches, no pipe, no sandals. No doubt about him.

So I stopped to talk. I introduced myself.

"Ken Holden!"

"Stan Plog!"

"Are you the guy who tried to start the Republican Club?" I asked.

"How did you know?"

"Just a guess."

Stan, born Stanley Mueller, was, like me, a child of the Depression, and a son of middle America. How he got to UCLA, and a career as

a behavioral psychologist, is one of the most unlikely life stories I've ever heard.

But I'll let Stan tell it in his own words, in a memoir that he wrote in his later years:

━ ━

I was born in the Los Angeles area but immediately was moved back to North Dakota to live with relatives because my father left at birth and my mother, Edith, couldn't afford to keep me during the Depression years.

I returned to California at about age eight when my mother remarried. My new dad, Clifton Plog, was a trombone player who worked with a number of dance bands in the Midwest and California. He gave me trombone lessons with the statement that I could avoid the poverty and makeshift life I faced until that time if I became a great trombonist—and did well in school. That was a clarion call to climb above some difficult beginnings. I disciplined myself practicing trombone religiously and changing my so-so grades in school to among the best in class.

It worked.

By my mid-teens I had my own twelve-piece dance band playing high school and college proms, weddings, bar mitzvahs, parties, the Pasadena Rose Queen Ball, and even coming close to capturing a TV show.

By the time I graduated from high school, I counted myself as one of the better trombonists in Los Angeles. On graduation night, I joined Dave Cavanaugh's band for stints that summer at the Salt-Air Ballroom outside of Salt Lake City and the Boardwalk in Santa Cruz, California.

I completed a year at Occidental College in Eagle Rock, California, on a music scholarship doing casuals (single music jobs), some motion picture and TV work, and juggling the demands of a full academic schedule and part-time employment to cover living expenses. At nineteen, I got an offer to join Horace Heidt's Orchestra as first trombone (my best music job ever!). Heidt had a very popular radio and TV show that featured young talent competing weekly for grand prizes awarded to a finalist every quarter. This job fulfilled all my expectations about how great life as a musician could be. It almost had too many benefits to count.

We toured the country about ten months a year, working one-nighters, seven nights a week with the chance to visit big and small towns in every mainland US state. Each week we did a simulcast radio and TV show, and I was featured on the theme song at the beginning and the end of every show ("On the Trail" melody from Ferde Grofé's *Grand Canyon Suite*). We even toured Europe and North Africa on a State Department goodwill tour, with a special concert in East Berlin when that city was still divided in four sectors. I still remember Communist bullies gathering around our bus after the concert and refusing to let us move out. Whenever we hit New York or Los Angeles, we did record dates and rehearsed new production numbers for shows we would take on the road.

I never faced a dull moment because each week we inserted routines for new talent into our road shows. The size of the crowds added to the excitement. I could not believe Mitchell, South Dakota, a small town then (1949–1950), it had the famous Corn Palace auditorium that could seat 3,200. We filled it for five nights with more people wanting to get in. Farm families drove more than one hundred miles to see us.

On a European tour in 1950, over ten thousand Germans crowded into the hall in Munich where Hitler had planned his big putsch while about three thousand more listened through speakers set up to the first American music they had heard since Hitler seized power.

Stan playing the trombone at one of his one-nighters somewhere in Southern California in the late 1940s.

Union scale included extras for traveling on the road, playing seven nights a week instead of six, the TV and radio weekly simulcast, and the recording dates. I added to my take-home pay by driving the wardrobe truck. I had to join the Teamsters Union to do that, but got paid only a pittance of scale. But that was fine. I liked to drive and the money added to everything else I earned.

A special relationship exists among musicians in most cases. They establish closer relationships than in most other professions I have observed. A lot of oddball and offbeat people exist, but all are accepted. Inside jokes are prevalent, often with a gallows humor focused around the difficult lives they face because they live precariously from one temporary job to another—and no pension plans. Those with the most musical talent become the de facto intellectual leaders in a band or orchestra. Others look up to them and respect their judgment but most musicians are very bright and creative.

However, this great life changed when the Korean War came along. I joined the 775th Air Force Band in Tucson, Arizona, in late November 1950, which gave me a chance to keep up my Hollywood musical contacts. It was a great choice, too. A bunch of talented young musicians also joined, all having the same idea—to be close to the Hollywood musical scene. The list included five-time Academy Award–winner John Williams, two future presidents of Local 47 of the musicians' union, a future arranger and tenor sax player with the Doc Severinsen Tonight Show band, and the lead alto from my teenage band. Friendships developed that last today.

After discharge I returned to Occidental College to continue pursuing a degree in music. I immediately got some good work around town—motion picture studio dates and weekend casuals. Soon I joined Freddy Martin's Orchestra on lead chair, a major recording artist at the time. This job proved a boon because I was married now with my wife expecting soon. And Freddy was a permanent fixture in the Cocoanut Grove ballroom at the Ambassador Hotel in Los Angeles. I could settle down and continue to attend Occidental. It required juggling my time carefully to meet the demands of a full-time job and a full academic load.

As perfect as everything seemed to be, nagging doubts arose over time about whether I really wanted to be a musician. Even while with Horace Heidt, I noticed that guys forty-five or older had trouble landing regular jobs. Bandleaders wanted young, fresh faces on the bandstand. That seemed crazy to me. In most professions at mid-career one can project future increased earning power, greater job stability, and more respect among peers. The temporariness and specialized roles of most gigs mean that one worries about the next job.

In short, I came to the conclusion that I loved music, but not the music business.

I decided to get out and leave a profession that had consumed my life for so many years, but offered a more limited future than I had imagined. This was a tough decision because I had devoted myself to it since I was almost nine, and I had no idea of what I might want to do. I had to support a family so I could not just drop everything and not earn a living. It was not made easier by the fact that my Mom and Dad both wished I would stay in music because of my success. My younger brother did, and is now the trumpet professor at the Staatliche Hochschule für Musik in Freiburg, and a classical composer. He enjoys it, but it's still difficult to make a substantial living for most musicians.

[Anthony Plog, Stan's brother, retired from the concert stage in 2001 to concentrate on composing. His works, mainly for brass, and including three operas, have been performed all over the world.]

At Occidental College, I sampled a lot of courses in search of a field that I would like. Many were interesting—biology, physiology, and even philosophy—but which career should I choose within any of these fields? I considered a pre-med major for a while, but dropped that. I thought marine biology was fascinating, but opted out after visiting an oceanographic institute and noticing the very limited lives that these people lived. What I seemed to like most was research—of all kinds. It meant discovering new things constantly. I looked into medical or physiological research, since it could combine a couple of my interests, but I came to the conclusion that this was not for me. I noticed that some people spent a lifetime in laboratories looking for a cure for a specific type of cancer but never came up with a solution. The wasted career in that kind of situation would seem depressing to me. My background in music to this point had built a need to find something that could provide a chance to work in an ever-changing environment.

Finally I sampled courses in the social sciences—abnormal and social psychology and sociology. The fields seemed fascinating though young in history and without lot of firm conclusions like the hard sciences. But they offered one advantage not available in the hard sciences. The student could jump around within the social sciences easily if current efforts did not seem intriguing or productive. The hard sciences proudly proclaim the precision and controls that define their experiments. For the most part, everything is done in laboratories where all elements of the design can be detailed and reported.

The social sciences do not enjoy such luxury. The behavior of people is complex and truly requires a social setting where it is impossible to nail down every variable to test hypotheses. Laboratory experiments using rats, chimps, and dogs never made sense to me. How can the reactions of animals to limited stimuli be interpreted as reflective of human behavior in social settings? To handle these kinds of difficulties the social sciences developed new and quite innovative research designs and advanced statistical procedures that seemed miles ahead of anything used in the hard sciences.

But I was unable to make up my mind as to what I wanted to do. Music is such a consuming and seductive passion that it's hard to leave the field. Most musicians stay on and become part-time real estate agents or travel agents to supplement their incomes, while still hoping for a big break. This was not for me. So I took time off from school to try to reach a conclusion during the year that Freddy Martin decided to spend a winter season at the Boca Raton Hotel in Florida, with a stop in Las Vegas to be featured with Elvis Presley, and one-nighters in between. I returned to Occidental and decided to concentrate on a degree in psychology. It would give me the most flexibility in what I could choose later, I believed, but I still had no clear idea of how I would use it. All I knew was that I would need a doctorate because a bachelor's degree would not buy entrance into any credible job.

At graduation, I applied to clinical psychology programs at a number of good schools, because I reasoned that I could always cross over to sociology or social psychology if I wished, but not the opposite since clinical psychology required "tickets"—my term for certification of psychologists by state review boards. The limitations of being a sideman musician prevented me from having lots of choices and I did not want that to happen again.

Surprisingly, Harvard University gave me the best scholarship deal. Their program emphasized training in all of the important social sciences, requiring students to pass qualifying exams both in a chosen field and in social psychology, sociology, and cultural anthropology. I accepted the offer and moved wife and child back to the Cambridge area. From that point on, it took me fifteen years to earn the same income in my new field as I did as a musician, not counting inflation, making my choice a bit sobering.

The first year at Harvard was fabulous! Exposure to great minds whose books I had read, deep immersion in multiple topics and fields of endeavor, new ideas through a ton of books we had to read each week, and exposure to fellow students who were so bright it was scary. It was a challenge just to keep up with the fast pace they established in class discussions and their ability to argue almost any point. I did not play my horn the first year to make certain I got through the qualifying exams, because we were told this was the flunk-out year, Indeed, and unfortunately, a lot of students didn't make the grade.

After the first year, I picked up my horn again to earn money and got the best work in town—North Shore Musical Theatre in the summer, more weddings and bar mitzvahs, and the plum job of all: Ruby Newman's Society Orchestra for society coming-out parties. Ruby's society events paid incredibly well, all compounded union scale. Jobs started at 10 p.m., with union scale beginning at 8:00 and going only until 11:00 p.m. After that point, scale increased to double time until we quit at 2:00 a.m. (we got extra as we had no intermissions). The band played continuously, because Boston society wanted their girls to always have someone to dance with and not have to sit around during intermissions. We also got travel time—to the North Shore where some of the big homes were located, or even flying to other locales for dates: Charleston, the Detroit area (for the Dodge family party), and more. I made lots of money while still attending grad school, a fact that also called into question my decision to leave music.

But my schooling from the second year was a different story. There were disappointments with Harvard. In course work and seminars, I was exposed primarily to more junior professors, many of whom were there on one-year assignments. They had little interest in teaching. Instead they focused primarily on their own research projects, hoping to create a reputation that would land them a good position at another university. They lampooned the older faculty whose reputations they would never achieve.

There was even greater disappointment in my clinical training. The psychiatrists who supervised our work seemed like they were from another planet. All adopted a Freudian perspective and many had a penchant for making wild, speculative assertions about what was going on in the lives of the cases were presented. I blew up in a couple of sessions with those respected therapists, commenting that the music field I left allows for free and creative artistic expression, but only within a foundation of understanding chord progression and having facility on an instrument. Psychiatry, in contrast, lacked a foundation for most of its undisciplined and unfettered speculation about people's lives. Surprisingly, I was not kicked out and somehow got through the courses. I thought of quitting and returning to a career in music, but finally took a different path. I latched onto the great names and each semester became a research and teaching assistant to such luminaries as Gordon W. Allport, Henry A. Murray, George A. Miller, and Jerry Bruner. Few people could match the personal qualities of Allport, and I chose him as my thesis adviser.

I served my clinical internship in the Department of Psychiatry at UCLA, and, after getting the doctorate, was offered a position at its Neuropsychiatric Institute as a medical psychologist. That was followed a year later by being named the academic director of a new program in social psychiatry, also within the Department of Psychiatry. The following year I was invited to establish and direct a new program to study urban social progress.

Nevertheless, contentment eluded me.

Academic life seemed to confining, with its focus on publishing (or perishing), and there always seemed to be a considerable amount of infighting among faculty members. It was not like the music business where players are collegial and accept all kinds of less-than-ideal conditions in their quest just to play their instruments.

I decided to go into business for myself.

That last, fateful sentence brings Stan to the first step on the journey that took us to Malibu and our three days with Ronald Reagan.

As for me, I too was a product of the Midwest: St. Joseph, Michigan, a small town (fewer than 8,500 people even today) on the shores of Lake Michigan and the St. Joseph River, a place so small that I remember we had only one policeman, known as Cookie the Cop to everyone. Most of the townspeople then (and for all I know nowadays too) were of German descent—and all my boyhood friends had German surnames.

In 1898, St. Joseph flirted briefly with a place in aviation history: A man named August Moore Herring took a motor-equipped glider to a nearby beach and kept it aloft for seven seconds. A few days later he tried again and stayed up for eleven seconds. But he never figured out how to control his rudimentary airplane, and the Wright brothers beat him to the laurels of the first heavier-than-air flight five years later. People in St. Joe didn't forget Mr. Herring and his quixotic brush with history, probably the only people other than a few aviation historians who remembered his name. I was born in 1927, the year Charles Lindbergh flew the Atlantic solo, and those two tenuous connections seemed to give me a romantic destiny. From the time I was little, I too wanted to fly. I wanted to have adventures. Small-town life was insufficient.

Not that I had any specific complaints. I had a great childhood in a great family in a great little town. And I look back with nothing but love at the America of my childhood, a country whose history was intimately bound to my family's. Look at the signatories of the 1638 Portsmouth Compact, when the Rhode Island followers of Anne Hutchinson declared their religious and political independence from the Massachusetts Colony, from the orthodoxies of the time, and you'll find the name Randall Holden. He was my ancestor, and he lived to be 80 in those short-lived times. So, yes, I come from good, hardy, self-reliant stock. And, like my ancestor, I never believed that something was right just because everybody around you thought it was. That trait of intellectual independence would get me in trouble when I embarked on an academic career, but it also led me into the orbit of Ronald Reagan.

My paternal grandfather, Perry Greeley Holden, had been born in 1865 right as the Civil War was ending. He was a professor of agronomy—one of the first, if not the very first—and had helped develop a strain of hybrid corn. He, too, was an impressive physical specimen; I remember him in his late seventies performing "skin the cat" on the horizontal bar, with his gold pocket watch swinging from his vest. Grandpa Holden remembered, as I now remember Pearl Harbor, Custer's Last Stand as if it had happened the day before. He was another reminder to me of our country's history, of my family's history. When Lincoln invoked "the mystic chords of memory, stretching from every battlefield and patriot grave," he could have been speaking of my family's heritage. It was something I learned to take very seriously as a young man—and still do.

My father, Ellsworth Holden, was superintendent of schools in our town—which sounds like it should have made my life easier, but of course it didn't. I've always joked that the children of school superintendents are the single most discriminated-against group of kids in America. The other kids automatically hate them, and teachers tend to handle them with kid gloves. My father defused any danger of favoritism—of teachers trying to get brownie points from him by coddling me or my brother—by gathering all of the staff together at the beginning of the school year and announcing: "Any teachers giving anything special to my sons in school will have to answer to me . . . and it won't be pleasant!" I didn't hear the story until years later, but it explained why some teachers acted as if they didn't like me and had it in for me in some way. In fact, it gave a free hand to those teachers who had any sort of grudge about how my father treated them—and were petty enough to take it out on an unsuspecting kid.

My father had been captain of the Michigan State wrestling team, and he had served rough duty in World War I on a seagoing Navy tug that specialized in hauling the hulks of torpedoed ships though the freezing North Atlantic and into safe haven in ports in Ireland. So he was a tough guy, a man's man. But he was also highly intelligent and educated, with a master's from Columbia University.

My mother, Marjorie, was a Baker from New York's Staten Island, part of a family that moved to Chicago, where, family legend said, they were friends with the Mrs. O'Leary whose cow was blamed for kicking over a lantern and starting the Great Fire of Chicago in 1871. I was never sure if the story was true, or if it was just a myth—especially because almost every family that had antecedents in Chicago claims to have had a connection with the poor woman. And no one blames Mrs. O'Leary or her cow anymore; the whole story was fabricated by a newspaper reporter who later admitted it was a work of journalistic fiction. I think I know how poor Mrs. O'Leary must have felt about being maligned by the press; in 1960s California I witnessed first-hand the way Ronald Reagan's speeches were cherry-picked for what we now call "gotcha!" moments while the great bulk of his political philosophy was caricatured by liberal reporters and their editors.

Mother had a very active, capable mind and was the most gregarious member of our family; she had many friends, both local and through extensive correspondence, writing and receiving letters all her life. I like to think she would have thrived in this Facebook era.

She was, however, mildly disappointed that I, her second and last child, hadn't turned out to be a girl. I remember she wanted me to play a musical instrument; I preferred to play baseball and football. If I'd taken her advice I might have had the same colorful life in music that Stan had—assuming I had a tenth of his musical talent, which of course I didn't.

My brother was, like my father, named Ellsworth. The name lasted until he joined the naval officer training program at Notre Dame. That's when a chief petty officer scowled at him: "That's a lousy name. From now on we'll call you Bill." So Bill he became, and Bill he stayed for the rest of his life. Unlike me, Bill, who was three years older, was laid back, uninterested in sports, and quiet. After the Navy, he became an aerospace engineer. I think in his mind I was always the aggravating, obnoxious younger brother.

Growing up in those days—and I think this is one of the things that has changed drastically and for the worse in our more lenient, post-Sixties culture—my brother and I, and every kid we knew as far as I can remember, were encouraged to be self-sufficient, to develop habits of independence and freedom at an early age. Let me give you an example: I had a paper route delivering the *Chicago Tribune,* a paper whose Sunday edition weighed exactly a ton. My parents didn't help; the paper route was my business, and it was up to me to deliver regardless of circumstance. And those circumstances could be rugged. My routine was to get up before dawn, ride my bike downtown to the distributorship, cut open bundles of the *Tribune,* fold as many copies as I had customers—sometimes fifty, sometimes up to one hundred— and fit them into the basket over my front wheel. Then it was back out into the still-dark morning, into rain, or snow, or whatever Michigan weather was throwing at us. Remember, it didn't get light until 8:30 or 9 a.m.—and school started at 8. So delivering the papers became a game of beat-the-clock, made especially difficult if weather conditions were such that it was too dangerous to ride the bike, and I had to walk it the length of my route.

But these responsibilities—and the refusal of my parents to coddle me in the slightest—helped develop habits of self-reliance and hardiness that helped me in life. There was something else, too: Being a member of the war class—my four years in high school coincided for the most part with the four years of World War II—I was part of an unusual generation of kids. We basically had no adolescence. Because of the war, there was a serious lack of men to do various important jobs. For instance, when I was fifteen, I had a job with the Indiana & Michigan Electric Co. driving a company car to calibrate and repair kilowatt-hour meters throughout Berrien County. The men who had done this job before the war had shipped out to someplace dangerous, and I felt I was helping them by holding the job down—but just until they came home, if by God's grace they did come home. Which not all of them did.

I also worked in the local shipyard installing radios in Army rescue boats. Some of my friends spent their evenings doing lab work on the metal characteristics of 105-mm shell casings. A local factory that had turned out women's hosiery before the war was now making parachutes. And remember, in the first years of the war, it wasn't certain that we would actually win it. We hoped we would; we were doing everything we could to win. Our country had been in wars before, but this was a new experience; this was a world war against ruthless enemies bent on our annihilation. The Japanese never attacked us in World War I. We were just high school kids, facing those awful realities. We had to grow up a lot faster than most kids—either now, or in the relatively carefree years before the war.

I have never doubted the benefits of my ancestry, the connection to the past, nor the small-town glories of St. Joe itself. I delivered newspapers and skated on frozen ponds, and I enjoyed the care of loving, if non-indulgent, parents. But I dreamed. I dreamed about flying and about how life might be different across the St. Joseph River, or across the Atlantic, or the broad Pacific. I listened to the radio broadcasts from Chicago and felt the same chill—the expectant something—that all kids of my generation felt at the wonder of the distant city and the magic of radio. In fact, I was so enamored of radio that I put together my own ham radio set and joined all the amateur clubs to learn Morse code. It turned out to be a useful skill, one that I put to use sooner than I expected.

When World War II came, I was thirteen, but I wanted to take part. I bore a personal grudge because George Jones, my friend and radio mentor, was killed at Pearl Harbor. George had enlisted in the Navy when he graduated from high school and because of his skill at Morse code was assigned to the destroyer USS *Downes,* which was in dry dock at Pearl Harbor. It was berthed right next to the battleship *Pennsylvania,* and another destroyer, USS *Cassin.* When the Japanese attacked on December 7, they badly damaged all three ships, although all survived to fight through the war, giving back much more than they had received. The headline in our town newspaper a few days later screamed "LOCAL BOY KILLED AT PEARL HARBOR." That was my friend, and that made the war personal for me, young as I was.

I was too young to contribute right away, but my longtime pal Shel Gates and I studied and got our commercial radiotelegraph licenses, and we were ready to leave for the West Coast the morning after our high school graduation. After three days westward on the Santa Fe Scout we arrived in San Francisco, checked in with the War Shipping Administration, and were immediately assigned ships. I got the SS *Nancy Hanks,* one of the famous Liberty ships, with a Navy crew to man the three-inch forward cannon, the five-incher on the stern, and the four 20 mm cannons lining the starboard side, likewise on the port side. Shel got the SS *Charles M. Russell,* another Liberty ship.

Everyone on board my ship had the same question: Who in hell was Nancy Hanks and how did she rate having a ship, even one as modest as ours, named for her? It was four months before we found out—she was Abe Lincoln's mother (and, to snap us into the present for a moment, she was purportedly a distant cousin, many times removed, of Hollywood star Tom Hanks).

It was late 1945, the fighting ferocious on Okinawa and the invasion of the Japanese home island set for November 1. The world was a very dangerous place. I was a ship's officer at only seventeen. The *Nancy Hanks* was carrying all the supplies of war in our holds and under our decks. In our overloaded tub, we zigzagged under radio silence across the Pacific, all alone (no convoys) in the vastness of the world's biggest ocean, waiting for a Japanese sub to spot us and torpedo us to kingdom come.

We relied on the expanse of the ocean to save us. We had orders to ignore any signals we might pick up from another Allied ship under attack. The thinking was that the Japanese might stick around after attacking one vessel to pick off any would-be rescuers. The *Nancy*

Hanks, lurching to the scene of a sub attack, would have made for easy pickings.

There was one other thing I took personally. There's a rule of the sea that says if a ship is sinking, the captain will be the last one to leave. However, the radio officer stays right there with him, sending out distress signals to anyone within range, right to the very end. I was the ship's radio officer. I found myself in the radio shack copying groups of five numbers from the Navy radio stations, then matching them with phrases in the code books. There I would be, at 0330 ship time, deep in the middle of the Pacific night, the only person on board who knew what was next for the *Nancy Hanks*. Words like responsibility and reliability suddenly took on new meaning.

My biggest scare—and remember, I was borderline scared anytime I allowed myself to think of exactly how far away I was from friendly old St. Joe—came one night at 0230 when the chief mate came down the ladder to me carrying a note that gave our present position. "Be ready to send this, Sparks!" he told me. One of our crew had spotted a reconnaissance plane that had been checking us out. They'd dropped a flare over the *Nancy Hanks*, and we'd spotted a light blinking on the horizon immediately thereafter. A Japanese sub? A patrol boat? A surface raider? Whatever it was, it was something we weren't going to enjoy meeting in the dark of night.

According to the ship's log, we started "violent evasive maneuvers."

What may have been the slowest vessel in the whole Pacific was engaged in "violent evasive maneuvers"? If you say so!

We spent a very tense night waiting for disaster to strike. Then the dawn came up, in Kipling's words, like thunder—and we saw the most beautiful sight!

Across the horizon, heading right toward us, there steamed an entire US Navy task force—aircraft carriers, battleships, cruisers, destroyers, more than we could have ever hoped for, enough to intimidate a small country and certainly more than any solitary Japanese attacker would have wanted to engage. Whatever was stalking us that night had the good sense to scuttle off into the vastness of the Pacific.

After twenty-eight days of that first voyage, we made landfall on Kwajalein in the Marshall Islands and then began a leisurely progress that took us to Leyte Gulf and from there to Lingayen Gulf in the Philippines. My shipmates and I took shore leave in places I'd never heard of before and found ourselves in situations that would have killed my parents (or at least my mother) if they'd ever known what their (not so much of a) baby boy was up to. But I held my own, and I grew up quickly. By the time I celebrated my eighteenth birthday somewhere on the waters between Manila and New Guinea, I had become a man. And I had discovered within myself a restlessness of spirit, a wanderlust that has never to this day gone away.

After the *Nancy Hanks,* I served on two more Liberty ships, but in the other direction—the Mediterranean, the Adriatic, Britain, and the Persian Gulf. Finally, I decided I had saved enough money to go to college. Along with my old pal Shel Gates, who had also served in the Merchant Marine, I applied to the University of Michigan at Ann Arbor. We were admitted and joined the crowd of ex-GIs there as part of the strangest nationwide freshman class in history. Thanks to the GI Bill, hundreds of thousands of recently discharged veterans were overrunning the campuses, swamping the kids who had just graduated from high school.

We were easily distinguished from the regular freshmen. For one thing most of us still wore some parts of our old uniforms. Gates and I still had our naval officer's long winter-rain overcoats, and our Navy blue pants. Others hung on to their field jackets and other items that were obviously government issue. It was a pattern you could see on any campus anywhere in the country.

Those poor kids straight from high school had a tough time, I realize now. They were thrown among guys just a few years older but with experience of the world that they couldn't even imagine. And the vets were serious men looking to make up for the years lost fighting the Nazis and the Japanese. The fraternities quickly dropped such frivolous traditions as "hell week" when freshman rushes were put through a series of humiliations before being initiated. After all, would some just-discharged marine who had endured the real hell of Iwo Jima really put up with this kind of nonsense? Instead, they had "work weeks" and "cleanup weeks" for their new members. The veterans weren't in college to party; they were there to get an education, graduate, and start their families. The professors were thrilled at this influx of serious students, as you can imagine.

I enrolled as an engineering student, but realized it wasn't for me. After two-and-a-half years, I came to the conclusion that I'd had it with higher education for the time being. There had been too many dull classrooms and not enough real life. And I missed real life, as hair-raising as it had been. I called home and told my father, "I'm going back to sea."

His answer: "I've been wondering how long you were going to last. I've seen it coming."

There was no, "You've got to stick with it," and no lecture about the importance of education. He knew me better than I knew myself.

So I headed to New York City where I checked in with the American Communications Association (ACA), which was the radio officers' union, and handled the assignments for guys like me. At the time, unfortunately, I discovered the union had been taken over by the Communists. That's no exaggeration for effect, either. I found out later that it had been founded by them; our president was an actual card-carrying party member.

I quickly realized something that Ronald Reagan was discovering in Hollywood, three thousand miles away and in a world far different from mine: Some unions were being run by people who had no love for America. I saw firsthand how the Reds took over union meetings and dominated the union although they formed just a minority of the membership.

Another thing I noticed: The Communist leadership of the union seldom took ship assignments; after all, if they were at sea they couldn't run the union for their own purposes.

When we did have meetings, they used the so-called "diamond formation" to make it look like they had more numbers on their side than they actually had. Here's how it worked: One member would sit up front in the center; another would sit in the center of the last row, and two others were midway up the sides. I soon joined the fight to oust the lefties from the union leadership and return it to its true membership. I did nothing heroic—just stuff like updating telephone lists of members we could trust and determining who was at sea or on vacation. Then I worked the phones to urge members to show up for meetings.

I'm glad to say we finally prevailed. One day we outvoted the Communists and booted the president.

That was an important lesson too: The Communists weren't unstoppable or inevitable. If good people joined together and tried hard, they could kick those bums out and preserve the freedoms they were so eager to take away. In 1950, the US Supreme Court put the final nail in the coffin of the Communists at the ACA; they had sued saying the anti-Communist provisions of the Taft-Hartley labor law—which required a loyalty oath—violated their First Amendment rights. It went all the way to the country's top court before they were finally rebuffed.

Education comes in strange forms. I got a good one learning the workings of the union and finding out that the leaders aren't necessarily representing the rank-and-file.

With the war over and a glut of qualified men looking for assignments, ships were hard to come by, but I got a plum assignment as radio officer on the SS *Bulkero,* a modern, twin steam-turbined gasoline tanker out of Port Arthur, Texas.

I thought we were just going to be sailing up and down the East Coast. I was wrong. I was about to embark on another adventure. The *Bulkero* headed to Cape Town, around the Cape of Good Hope and up into the Persian Gulf, through the Suez Canal to England. Our voyage eventually took us to Ceylon (now Sri Lanka), Hong Kong (then under British control), Shanghai (very much an international city back then), Manila (only recently granted its freedom from America)—and back to San Diego. During the voyage, the ship was set on fire once, ran aground once, got gasoline in the drinking water (we had to rig canvas to catch rainwater to drink), and had a near-mutinous crew. To cap it off, when we got to San Diego, we got a new captain. He was 350 pounds and enthusiastically gay; every halfway decent-looking man on the crew had to spend the rest of the voyage trying to fend him off. Yes, I know, it sounds like a bad novel—although a bad novel somehow would have included a beautiful island girl who found radio officers irresistible.

But my island girl was still a few years in my future.

Then, North Korea invaded South Korea, and I got a draft notice. Never mind that I'd already been in serious harm's way once (the Merchant Marine had the second highest casualty rate in World War II, after the Marine Corps). I looked at the draft notice, stuck it in my pocket, and went to the nearest Air Force recruiting station. I still had my old dream of flying. And thanks to those North Koreans, here was my chance, I thought. I enlisted and told them I wanted to be a pilot.

When the Air Force officers' board asked me, "Why do you want to join the Air Force?" I had my answer ready.

"In World War II," I told them, trying to act as if what I said was spontaneous, not rehearsed a hundred times, "I was on a ten-knot Liberty ship and a sitting duck. The next time I want to be in an F-86, shooting back."

They loved that answer, as you might expect. But then came the physical. My eyesight, it turned out, was 20-30, and in those days you needed to be 20-20. I was disqualified from flight training. Instead, the Air Force sent me to a yearlong radar and high-altitude bombardment course. I graduated first in my class—and then they shipped me to Mathers AFB near Sacramento and put me to work running a maintenance shop. By the time I got out in 1954, I was a staff sergeant—and I had met the island girl of my dreams.

Here's how that came about: The Air Force had a program called Operation Boot Strap, under which airmen who were shy of their college degrees could go to school while still serving. By now I was interested in psychology, and I enrolled at San Fernando Valley State College, the same school where I would wind up as an assistant professor. (It's now called California State University at Northridge.) I was splitting my days between my Air Force work, which ran from 3:30 p.m. to 11:30 p.m., and my full-time course work, when I met my Julie—in an abnormal psychology class if you can believe it. As good a way as any, I say, to meet the love of your life.

Our first conversation took place when she approached me to buy tickets to some college event. I was impressed immediately. She was a beautiful Hawaiian/Caucasian girl, with a humorous, self-possessed look and a kind of gentle firmness and competence. Whatever the tickets were for, I remember I didn't buy any.

But I did ask her out.

We were married in 1952, raised two great kids (my son Keali'i teaches in Hawaii; my daughter Wailani is retired in Oregon with her ex-Navy husband), and celebrated our golden anniversary. I lost Julie after fifty years of marriage, and I'm still trying to adjust to that. I doubt if I ever will.

So there you have the gypsy, the dreamer, the unsettled soul who found himself teaching in UCLA in 1960. I was, of course, miserable.

The atmosphere at UCLA didn't just tilt liberal; it was, to my point of view, poisonously left-wing. When Stan and I tried to start conservative study groups, we were treated like lepers. The administration denied us promotions that we felt we deserved. Well-meaning friends advised us to lie low. In this season, openly Republican, openly conservative scholars were considered, to borrow a phrase from our ideological foes, enemies of the people. And it would only get worse as the '60s progressed.

In our case, it wasn't simply a matter of collegial disagreement or being ostracized from the tenured fraternity. It was much worse than that. We were the recipients of outright threats. I remember a supervisor telling me, more in sorrow than in anger, "Ken, you meet all the requirements for advancing to associate professor . . . but you just don't *look* like an associate professor." In other words, the crew cut and the rest of my appearance marked me as politically unreliable. A pair of granny glasses and a set of muttonchops would have opened a lot of doors. A poncho and a pair of bell bottoms—a shame that I didn't borrow some from the Navy during my Merchant Marine days—might have landed me a full professorship.

Sometime in 1962 or '63, Stan and I decided we had to find something else that would give us some professional leverage to arrange our own economic safety. We needed a reliable financial cushion to protect us against the possibility of a punitive administrative backlash. It was clear that we couldn't depend on the so-called tolerance of academia.

So we decided to start our own consulting business.

But how? What could a couple of clinical psychologists—whose strength lay mostly in abstract and theoretical speculation about behavioral norms—actually do in the real world? This was a puzzle.

One day, the solution presented itself. It came in the form of a complicated clinical case at the NPI. Stan was asked to evaluate the intelligence of a grammar-school child diagnosed as retarded by someone—and it could have been almost anyone because they weren't properly trained—at a local school district. The girl, blind from birth, had been born prematurely to an American GI and his Korean wife.

By this time, we had seen case after case of incompetent pedagogues making inaccurate diagnoses about students—mostly as a matter of their own convenience. If a child didn't do well, they labeled him or her as retarded (a word that came to have damaging implications and would be refined later to "learning disabled" or some other less onerous category), so that they could banish their own failures into one group. These diagnoses didn't take into account dyslexia, poor eyesight, deafness, or any other consideration now part of the modern diagnostic techniques.

It turns out that the diagnosis of the child as retarded had been made by an undertrained part-time psychologist working in one of the many underserved California school districts. The girl's parents accepted the diagnosis. It was, they thought, punishment for getting married against the wishes of both families. Primitive superstition joined with dumb bureaucracy to ruin a little girl's life.

Stan—who had by then earned his doctorate from Harvard—was in charge of the evaluation at NPI, and he gave the girl a full battery of IQ and cognitive function tests. His conclusion: Not only was she not retarded, she had an IQ of 125—well above average. However, because she had never been placed in special education classes for the blind, she was unable to demonstrate her true capabilities. It was the system—we both concluded—that was retarded, not the child.

Furious, Stan explained to the parents that the child's blindness didn't result from any sin, ethical flaw, or flouting of social conventions. Her condition had developed because incompetent doctors at the Air Force Hospital, after delivering the child prematurely, pumped too much oxygen into her incubator, rupturing the blood vessels in her eyes. The only thing she needed to be successful was the right kind of care.

We were pretty convincing, and, needless to say, the child blossomed at the Braille Institute.

For us, it was further proof, if any proof were needed, that the system was profoundly defective. Groups of so-called social engineers, complicating any reasonable approach to large problems, inevitably screwed up even simple tasks—*especially* simple tasks.

At the same time, a lightbulb went off. Here was our opportunity. A great part of the problem lay in the initial diagnosis. Careless, untrained psychologists were quick to misread the problem of the little blind girl. We had to get at the root of the difficulty, which was, after all, just a technical problem.

The school districts in the greater Los Angeles area lacked sufficient finances to provide well-trained, full-time psychological support. Their lack of funds made them dependent on part-time help that was, in too many cases, unqualified. Psychological evaluations had become a kind of rough, drive-by system. All we had to do was to find some way to provide first-rate, dedicated psychological support and—no small feat!—keep the costs down.

At the time, thirty-two small school districts in the greater Los Angeles area were receiving the equivalent of only half a day, every other week, of psychological services from the county. This provided a base that we could work with, and our solution was relatively simple. We had access to a lot of first-rate, highly qualified, underemployed psychologists at the university. They would welcome the professional credit, not to mention the extra income of a part-time job serving the school districts. We could pick, recruit, and train our own psychologists and employ them in the field—university-trained professionals making periodic visits to the outlying districts. Not just quick drive-by evaluations, but select and healthy assessments.

There was no doubt that we could, by our own educated oversight, maintain quality control, and that would eliminate the unsupervised aspect of the evaluations. There would be other benefits as well. The school districts, under our system, would save the expenses of office space, secretaries, vacations, sick leave, health care, pensions, and so on—all of which they would have to pay if obliged to hire even part-time psychologists.

So we plunged into the psychological evaluation field; we went through all the requirements of licensing and approval and became independent contractors—technically not connected to the university but able to employ a lot of the university's facilities.

We called ourselves University Consultants Inc. and were, from the first, a fine success. Soon we were deploying a small army of part-time psychologists. Our services made the remote school districts happy, and it made us even happier—we were more independent. We were on the winning side of a complex issue. And we were doing God's work, saving little kids from the indifference of uncaring bureaucracy and helping them make something of their lives.

University Consultants was such a success that we saw we could branch out, providing our services to private industry as well as to government agencies. We changed the name of the company to Behavior Science Corporation (BASICO); it sounded more impressive and punchy, and the new name distanced us even further from the taint of academia and thrust us further out into the real world.

Business leaders began hiring us to evaluate programs and staff, to explain why they might run a company a certain way, to evaluate candidates for promotion, to advise them about the benefits and problems of mergers, to observe board meetings and see how they were conducted. Job candidates began using the word "plogging" as shorthand for the process through which Stan and I put them.

As word got out, BASICO had become a recognized consulting firm with some clout. By the mid '60s, we had expanded into politics, my favorite field. We asked questions, we did in-depth surveys, we published studies that sought to clarify the issues that politicians and their handlers and consultants had been wrestling with since the birth of the Republic. Why do people vote for certain candidates? What turns people for or against certain candidates? In the midst of all the issues that spring up like weeds during an election, which are the ones that *really* affect voters' choices. At the time, it was groundbreaking work. Nowadays, of course, no one makes a decision of any kind in this area without first consulting the consultants.

As we expanded and got a reputation for good work, I was even invited to the Pentagon to brief the staff of Joint Chiefs of Staff on a situation that had unexpectedly sprung up in the military. It was losing experienced officers at a very fast clip and wanted us to find out why there had been so much leakage into private industry. After all, there was a war going on in Vietnam, and, while it doesn't make sense to civilians, combat duty—if you survive it—is one of the great ways to get on the up escalator in the military. So what was happening? Was it disillusionment with the military life? Was it fear of death or dismemberment (which would not have been unreasonable)? Or was the military doing something wrong to drive out these junior and mid-rank officers—captains, majors, and lieutenant colonels— who could be, if they stayed, the Eisenhowers and Pattons of the next generation?

We opened an office for marketing and research in D.C., and went to work on the problem. As we investigated, the answer became pretty obvious. Primarily, it was an issue of dislocation. Military officers hadn't counted on the disruptive effects of so many service transfers on their families. They found that when they reached a certain age—usually in their 30s, a time when they would settle down in civilian life—the military uprooted the entire family and moved them to a new duty station. That same havoc repeated itself over and over so that during a twenty- or thirty-year military career an officer could expect to change his home base half a dozen times. That meant constant turnover for everyone in the family: new schools, new friends, and, in many cases, new careers for the spouse. The military hadn't foreseen the emotional toll of such frequent relocations. They didn't factor in the ultimate bitterness of broken marriages, lost friendships, overall tension.

There were easy solutions: reenlistment contracts that provided guaranteed periods in one station; efforts not to chop up a child's education and to take into account the individual price of a transfer.

It took some effort—the military is famously bullheaded in making adjustments, and there was a kind of hard-headed stubbornness to the advocates of the "no man is indispensable" tradition—but eventually compromises were made. Within the boundaries of military needs, reforms allowed for the retention of essential officers by bending policies. Of course, that was then. I suspect that this is a problem that never gets solved permanently, especially in times of war.

Around this time, too, we met the man who knew the man who would eventually give us our brush with history.

Dr. Robert W. Krueger, a physicist and committed conservative, had left the Rand Corporation to start the Planning Research Corp. think tank. He had deep connections in the Republican State Central Committee—an important conservative resource. Nowadays, there are many think tanks and fund-raising groups that serve the same purpose, but this was an early Wright Brothers attempt to fly. Planning Research maintained contact with important GOP donors, laid out Republican and conservative positions, and vetted would-be candidates.

Sometime in the course of 1965, Krueger asked Stan to write some position papers for the statewide Republican committee.

There was a good reason that we began consulting for Krueger, and, as I think about it, why I went to hear Reagan that night in the valley: BASICO was doing just fine, Stan and I were making money, but I had an unsettled feeling about the nature of our mission. It should be about more than making us independent, both personally and financially, from the academic world. We were both advocates—passionate advocates—for the cause of conservative Republicanism. What we needed was a focus.

It was at that ripe moment that I went to see Reagan speak at the schoolhouse in Westwood. I couldn't get over that he bothered to present such a meticulous, airtight case for conservatism to a handful of followers in a little backwater classroom.

The next day I told Stan about my epiphany. He was impressed. And Stan didn't impress easily. Of the two of us, he was the one with the most political fire in his belly; unlike me, he actually thought Barry Goldwater was a little squishy.

It turns out that I wasn't the only one who had seen the high potential in Ronald Reagan. The State Republican Party—as well as a group of private supporters, the Friends of Ronald Reagan—had already been monitoring him and pushing him to run for office.

The California Republicans were, however, a house badly divided.

5

The Split

We were worried about the Democrats, but not as worried as we were about our fellow Republicans. With a little luck, and a few more of Governor Pat Brown's patented gaffes, we could handle the Democrats, we thought. It was our own party—the Republicans—that gave us the willies.

By late '65, California Republicans were waging a nasty civil war. As in all such wars, it pitted the old against the new, the moderate Establishment Republicans versus the fiery conservative Young Turks. The clash was inevitable after the thumping that Barry Goldwater took in the '64 presidential race. Bitter feelings and smoldering grudges littered the field. Someone had to answer for such a crushing defeat.

Before that crucial election, Eastern moderates had dominated the Republican Party. New York State's liberal governor Nelson Rockefeller was the front runner for the presidential primary election in '64. However, in '61 he had divorced his first wife and married Margaretta "Happy" Murphy, who had herself divorced to marry the governor. All might have been forgiven, but on the eve of the presidential primary, Happy gave birth to Nelson Rockefeller Jr. For Rockefeller, the timing couldn't have been worse; it reminded GOP stalwarts why they didn't like Rocky. "Have we come to the point in our life as a nation where the governor of a great state—one who aspires to the nomination for president of the United States—can desert a good wife, mother of his grown children, divorce her, then persuade a young mother of four children to abandon her husband . . . and marry the governor?" raged US Senator Prescott Bush of Connecticut, the father and grandfather of two future Republican presidents.

Republican women branded Rockefeller a "wife stealer." He was booed at the convention in the Cow Palace. The nomination went to Barry Goldwater, who, after being branded an extremist, delivered a defiant acceptance speech: "I would remind you," he said, "that extremism in the defense of liberty is no vice."

Goldwater, who had an endearing, if reckless, habit of speaking off-the-cuff, had once told a news conference that "this country would be better off if we could just saw off the Eastern Seaboard and let it float out to sea." Not wise. He also called for the privatization of Social Security, the elimination of welfare, and leaving civil rights to the individual states. He had voted against the Civil Rights Act.

Those positions, which seemed extreme to the vast middle, along with Johnson's aggressive campaign—a famous TV ad showed a child picking the petals from a daisy during a nuclear countdown that ended in a mushroom cloud—proved decisive. The outcome was a landslide. Johnson carried forty-four states, while Goldwater carried six, mostly in the Deep South. No surprise there.

Naturally, there was a wide divergence of opinion in California about what exactly went wrong and how to carry on. As it happened, a neat geographical split defined the warring sides. The Old Guard held the northern part of the state—everything above Bakersfield. Embedded in the San Francisco Bay Area, they had old money, tradition, no broken crockery, and a reputation for moderation, a conciliatory Rockefeller-style approach to politics.

On the other side stood the Young Turks, who held the southern part of the state, rambunctious children of Barry Goldwater and the Orange County arch-conservatives. They were the muscular Republicans, dismissing every gesture of political conciliation—another name, in their eyes, for appeasement. Hardheaded self-made businessmen, they believed in the most elemental and purest version of capitalism. What they saw in the cultural drift of the party was the eventual destruction of the free-market system—and the growing tyranny of the counterculture frustrated and infuriated them. They resolutely wanted to avoid the clutches of an already bloated government. They didn't want to watch their world undone by an abject surrender to a spoiled generation of entitlement addicts. The oil wildcatters, media tycoons, automobile barons, retail giants, and insurance magnates had sworn themselves enemies of the welfare state—and they were itching for a fight.

As luck would have it, a clash was looming on the horizon.

After the catastrophe of the '64 presidential race, the two-term incumbent Democrat governor, Edmund G. "Pat" Brown, announced that he planned to run for reelection in '66.

Brown had been involved in California politics for what seemed forever. His first campaign (for the State Assembly) was in 1928! Calvin Coolidge was president at the time, and even in 1966 that seemed a very long time ago indeed. In fact, it was so long ago that Brown was a Republican at the time. It wasn't until 1950, though, that he actually got elected to something, when he became attorney general. By this time he was a Democrat and moving more and more toward the liberal end of the spectrum. He was elected governor for the first time in 1958.

From this point in history, so many decades later, I find it fascinating to look at the biographical similarities between Pat Brown and Ronald Reagan and speculate about the family influences that drove them to succeed. Their differences were great, of course, but picture this: They had both had out-of-control Irish Catholics fathers who

73

married Protestant women of far greater probity. They both started out at one end of the ideological spectrum but found a home at the other.

Brown's mother, Ida Shuckman, was a first-generation German Protestant. His father, Edmund Joseph Brown, was an Irish-Catholic immigrant. They produced four children; their first, Edmund, arrived on April 21, 1905.

Like young Ronald Reagan, young Edmund Brown grew up in a household where Reformation and Counter-Reformation coexisted in uneasy peace. His father wanted the kids to go to Mass and attend Catholic schools. His mother adamantly insisted that they shouldn't. Nelle Reagan won the religious wars in her house; Ida Brown had to settle for a draw. Eventually she and her husband divorced, and the religious gulf between them was one of the reasons.

Young Edmund handled the whole issue by declaring himself a noncombatant; he became an agnostic and stayed that way until 1938, when he rediscovered his father's religion and became a devout Catholic.

Like Jack Reagan, Brown's father was charming, boisterous, larger than life. He had, by all accounts, a gift for the blarney, a fondness for whiskey, and a compulsive dream of making a better life for himself and his family. Like Jack Reagan, he kept trying to start his own business.

Ida, like Nelle and so many other women of that era, had a passion for the better things in life. She liked politics, and she liked literature. While her husband was going wild—and a man of substance could go very wild in turn-of-the-century San Francisco—Ida dragged her sons, Edmund and Harold, to lectures and political rallies.

Unlike Jack Reagan, Edmund Brown had some success in business—or, rather, in businesses. He started a photo studio, a penny arcade, a movie theater, and a novelty store. By 1911, he was a well-known figure in post-quake San Francisco. But like Jack Reagan, he had a fatal flaw. Jack's was the booze; Edmund's was gambling. By

1912, he had been cleaned out, and his boys, who were mere children, had to go to work.

Young Edmund was just seven years old at the time. He started as a newspaper boy selling the *Chronicle* and the *Examiner,* then became an usher at a movie theater, sold sodas, took pictures of tourists, and hustled holiday cards at Christmas. But, horrified by his father's feckless life and the damage it was doing to the family, he began looking for something else.

Education, he decided—with his mother's guidance—offered a way out of the back-alley hustling that had become his father's legacy to the family. Make no mistake, though, he did learn from his father: Learning to make deals as he hustled for a buck was great training for a future politician.

Brown excelled in high school, both academically and outside the classroom. He played soccer, he founded a fraternity that was half Jewish and half Gentile, and he involved himself in every extracurricular activity he could find. He also earned his lifelong nickname there when he ended a war bonds speech by declaiming Patrick Henry's immortal quote, "Give me liberty or give me death!"

When he graduated, though, there was a problem: His family couldn't afford to send him to college, so he went to work for his father again, managing his cigar store while running a dice game of his own. Once again, though, the player's life didn't appeal to him; he enrolled in the San Francisco College of Law. He became a top student while working days and attending classes at nights. He passed the bar in 1927 and in 1929 eloped with Bernice Layne, his high school sweetheart. He practiced law; fathered a family, including Jerry, another future governor of California; and began his long journey to Sacramento.

Brown started out running for the Assembly as a Republican— and went down in flames, nabbing a mere five hundred votes. Gradually he began his transition toward the Democrats, and in 1934 he switched parties officially. In 1939 he ran for district attorney in San Francisco and lost again, but ran again in and won.

Brown embarked on a campaign to clean up the DA's office and the city. The racketeer's son became a racket-buster, even closing down his father's gambling den. He also prosecuted pornographers, abortionists, and bookies. He made a reputation for himself as—the words are his own—"a mean little bastard."

In 1946, the "mean little bastard" made his first attempt at statewide office, running for attorney general of California. It was a repeat of the San Francisco race—he lost the first time out, then ran again four years later and won.

And again he repeated the pattern of his days as San Francisco DA, running down mobsters, pornographers, and corrupt politicians. As the only Democrat in statewide office, he became the party's bright hope to take the governor's mansion.

To do that, though, he had to get past Goodwin Knight, the Republican governor. And he didn't think he could manage that. Knight was popular—and Democrats had only held the governorship once so far in the twentieth century. That governor was Culbert Olson, a left-wing Mormon-turned-atheist defeated after one term by Earl Warren.

Then fate intervened in the person of US Senate Minority Leader William F. Knowland. A Republican, Knowland decided to quit his Senate seat and the considerable power that came with being minority leader and run for governor in 1958. He basically bullied Knight out of running for reelection.

Brown and his people knew an opportunity when they saw it. Three weeks after Knowland announced his candidacy, Brown announced his and proceeded to wage a bare-knuckle campaign that Knowland couldn't counter.

Knowland, Brown charged, was a right-wing extremist. He was an opportunist who wanted to use Sacramento as a springboard to the

White House. Brown ran as what he called "a responsible liberal"—an inoffensive centrist, in other words—and he beat Knowland by a million votes, dealing a death blow to any plans Knowland had of one day being president.

Once in office, Brown shocked everyone, supporters and opponents alike, by embarking on an ambitious plan of change. In 1959, he enacted a series of laws, including the Fair Employment Practices Act banning discrimination in the workplace; set up a consumer protection agency; and got funding to build spectacular new infrastructure: highways, bridges, rail systems, waterways, and schools.

In 1960, he pushed through a bond measure that raised billions of dollars—and in 1960, a billion dollars was not a number to be bandied about lightly—to bring water from Northern California to Southern California. He also got his Master Plan for Education passed, creating new campuses for the University of California.

Brown appeared to be running the table, but his first term also contained some of the seeds for his eventual fall. The first crack in Brown's façade was his mishandling of the Caryl Chessman case.

Let me get something out of the way here: Chessman, like me, was born in St. Joseph, Michigan. Yes, it was a small town. But, no, I didn't know him. Nor would I brag about it if I did.

A petty criminal and lowlife, Chessman was convicted in California of being the so-called "Red Light Bandit," who stalked people in isolated places, like parks and lovers' lanes, brandishing a red light that made them think he was a police officer. Then he robbed them, and, in the case of women victims, raped them.

What Chessman hadn't counted on was California's so-called "Little Lindbergh" law, which called for the death penalty for kidnapping. The fact that he had dragged some of his women victims some distance from their cars to violate them was enough to get him convicted of kidnapping. And it was enough to get him sentenced to death in 1948.

Chessman lingered on Death Row for almost a dozen years, the longest such stretch at that time. He wrote a couple of books that pleaded his case (he maintained his innocence, with only the slightest justification), and gradually built up sympathy. His case became a cause célèbre not only in California but around the world. Had he been executed in 1948, of course, none of this would have happened, and his name wouldn't even be remembered by the time Pat Brown got around to dealing with him.

Here's where Brown's divided personality got him in trouble. He had been a remorseless prosecutor and as governor had to decide fifty-nine times whether to grant clemency to a state prisoner scheduled for execution. He commuted the sentences of twenty-three and sent thirty-six to the gas chamber. His conversion to Catholicism gradually led to opposition to the death penalty at a time when most Americans regarded it as a just end for murderers.

Chessman, however, hadn't actually killed anyone; he was on Death Row for kidnapping. After numerous appeals and eight postponements, his date with the gas chamber was approaching. Jerry Brown convinced his father to grant Chessman another sixty-day stay and try to get the State Legislature to pass a moratorium on the death penalty.

Brown, confident in his ability to get whatever he wanted from the Legislature (after all he was forty-three for forty-four in getting approval of his major reform proposals), sent a high-minded message asking for the moratorium. "The death penalty has been a gross failure," Brown wrote. "Beyond its horror and incivility, it has neither protected the innocent nor deterred the wicked. The recurrent spectacle of publicly sanctioned killing has cheapened human life and dignity without the redeeming grace which comes from justice meted out swiftly, evenly, humanely."

For once, the Legislature wasn't buying it, and the state Supreme Court refused to overturn Chessman's sentence. Brown dithered some more, then declined to give him executive clemency, and on May 2, 1960, Caryl Chessman entered the gas chamber.

He almost made it out again, too. A judge had issued yet another stay of execution. But his secretary misdialed the warden's number. When the secretary did get through, the gas pellets had already been dropped. "It's too late," the warden said: Whoever opened the door to remove Chessman would be exposed to the same fumes that he was inhaling. It was enough that Caryl Chessman, robber, kidnapper, rapist, was asphyxiating. No one else needed to join him.

The Chessman case did considerable damage to Brown's reputation. The radical left turned on him—as they always tend to turn on the merely liberal—and conservatives thought he had displayed weakness of character in his vacillation over Chessman's fate.

For the first time, Brown, who had seemed untouchable, lost political capital, all in the cause of a lowlife who wasn't worth the time of day.

More bad news was to come for Brown. The 1960 Democratic Convention in Los Angeles should have been a crowning moment for the governor. After all, he was one of the Democrats' brightest stars—and California's favorite son—or had been until he'd bungled the Chessman case. When he appeared at the convention, however, he was booed by delegates who opposed the death penalty.

Then he made an even bigger blunder. He was supposed to bring the California delegation into line behind John F. Kennedy, but somehow he lost control. The delegates split three ways, although they eventually came together for Kennedy's candidacy. Brown, on the national stage for the first time, looked like an ineffective bungler. His indecisiveness earned him the nickname "Tower of Jell-O."

By all the rules of politics, Brown's career should have been on the downslide. But in 1961, looking ahead to the 1962 race, he reinvented himself, as they say nowadays. His advisers coached him on how to excel on TV—lose the eyeglasses, be more expressive, wear lighter-colored suits (after all, this is sunny California). He lost weight and went on a statewide talking tour, stirring up the base and reminding people of all he had done for them.

Then came 1962, and a truly dangerous opponent: former vice president Richard Nixon.

Nixon was a native Californian who could practice knee-in-the-groin politics with the best of them. His first run for public office in 1946 had come out of the blue. The Republicans were looking for a candidate to run against Democratic representative Jerry Voorhis, an idiosyncratic New Dealer who nevertheless kept getting reelected by comfortable margins in a heavily Republican district in what was then a largely rural swath of Los Angeles County. No one seemed capable of unseating Voorhis until Herman Perry, the Bank of America branch manager in Whittier, suggested Nixon, a family friend with whom he had served on the Whittier College Board of Trustees before the war.

Nixon was a Navy lawyer, a lieutenant commander based in Baltimore, when he got the call. He flew to California, met with the GOP committee, got their approval, and resigned his commission. The rest was history. Nixon retired Voorhis. Comfortably reelected in '48 (he actually won both the Democratic *and* Republican primaries), he then decided to run for the Senate.

Nixon's opponent was Representative Helen Gahagan Douglas, a former opera singer, movie actress, and New Deal warrior, who had served three terms in Congress (during which she carried on a very public affair with fellow rep Lyndon Johnson). Douglas was highly unpopular, even among mainstream Democrats, especially after a vicious primary campaign, as the following excerpt from *RN: The Memoirs of Richard Nixon* indicates:

One afternoon in 1950, I was working in my office when Dorothy Cox, my personal secretary, came in and said, "Congressman Kennedy is here and would like to talk to you."

Jack Kennedy was ushered in and I motioned him into a chair. He took an envelope from his breast pocket and handed it to me. "Dick, I know you're in for a pretty rough campaign," he said, "and my father wanted to help out."

We talked for a while about the campaign. As he rose to leave, he said, "I obviously can't endorse you, but it isn't going to break my heart if you can turn the Senate's loss into Hollywood's gain."

After he left I opened the envelope and found it contained a $1,000 contribution. Three days after I won in November, Kennedy told an informal gathering of professors and students at Harvard that he was personally very happy that I had defeated Mrs. Douglas.

Nixon and Douglas went after each with bared teeth. But it was another candidate in the Democratic primary race, Manchester Boddy, editor and publisher of the *L.A. Daily News*, who provided both sides with their most cutting gibes. His newspaper dubbed Douglas "The Pink Lady," because of her left-wing connections. It was also he who coined the immortal sobriquet "Tricky Dick" for Nixon. In the general election campaign, both sides gleefully appropriated Boddy's insults and used them unsparingly. Even as Nixon portrayed Douglas as being too far left to represent the people of California, she, according to some accounts, referred to him as "the young man in the black shirt." In other words: a Nazi.

Three decades later, Douglas mentioned in her memoirs that Ronald Reagan was among those who worked hard for her. She had it wrong. He had actually started out favoring her, but when Nancy Davis, then his girlfriend, took him to a Nixon rally, he was impressed by the young congressman and quietly switched allegiance, even raising funds for Nixon.

Nixon, of course, didn't linger long in the Senate. In 1952, Dwight Eisenhower asked him to be his running mate, and he became vice president for two terms, earning a formidable reputation as an anti-Communist and a promoter of American values overseas and in many ways as the first modern vice president.

Nixon's first defeat came in 1960 at the hands of the same Jack Kennedy who had slipped him the envelope full of cash a decade earlier. But it was close. Kennedy only won by 120,000 votes nationwide—about 0.2 percent—with allegations of voter fraud in both Texas and Illinois, which Kennedy won. Nixon declined to contest the results, and Kennedy was inaugurated without further ado.

After the election defeat, Nixon returned to California, practiced law, wrote a book, and only very reluctantly agreed to challenge Pat Brown.

Once again, as had happened four years before, Brown had a seemingly formidable opponent with a fatal flaw—the same fatal flaw that Knowland had. He could be accused of running for governor of California only to position himself for a run at the White house.

Brown's people waged a ruthless campaign: They portrayed Nixon as a right-wing loony (never mind that many conservatives didn't consider him one of their own); they called him a carpetbagger who hadn't lived in California in almost a decade; they suggested he was mentally unstable; they hinted that he had a drinking problem. In other words, they demolished him personally to defeat him politically. And it worked.

In the end, Brown won the state race by nearly 300,000 votes, more than Kennedy's margin of victory nationwide in 1960. The defeat left Nixon so dispirited that he famously told the press: "You won't have Nixon to kick around anymore because, gentlemen, this is my last press conference."

That decisive victory made Brown such a favorite of the national Democrats that he was for a while the favorite to be Johnson's running mate in 1964, a job that eventually fell to Hubert H. Humphrey.

Both Knowland and Nixon would have some measure of revenge in 1966, working tirelessly behind the scenes on behalf of Ronald Reagan's campaign to oust their old nemesis.

Pat Brown had enacted equal rights laws, built superhighways, and, through a series of dams and pipelines, moved billions of gallons of water from the rainy north of the state to the parched south. Although a backer of the death penalty when he was a prosecutor, he began to question it as governor. At the beginning of his second term, he was the most popular politician in the state and looked unbeatable.

But four years is a long, long time in politics. During Brown's second term, the world changed—California leading the way—and he didn't seem to know how to the deal with it.

For one thing, the campuses exploded, starting with the University of California at Berkeley. The public face—and voice—of the Berkeley rebellion was a New Yorker named Mario Savio, who had started there in 1963. Abandoning the Catholic faith of his Italian-American childhood, he quickly became intoxicated by the spirit of rebellion he found at Berkeley. His first demonstration was a boycott of Mel's Drive-In, a burger joint owned by Harold Dobbs. What was Mr. Dobbs's great offense? He was running for mayor of San Francisco as a Republican. That couldn't be tolerated in Berkeley—no matter how tasty his burgers.

Savio's first arrest came in 1964 when he and his comrades picketed the venerable Sheraton Place Hotel to pressure it to hire more black people in visible jobs. There was an added incentive for Savio— a young woman whom he had met in class and had become highly attracted to was one of the demonstrators.

Savio spent the summer of 1964 in Mississippi registering black voters as part of the Mississippi Freedom Summer. At the end of the

project—and after a few hairy encounters with local segregationists—
he was asked to stay on as an organizer in Mississippi, but decided
instead to go back to Berkeley. There, things were coming to a boil.

The proximate cause of the outburst at Berkeley—long the site of
agitation about this or that pet cause, opposition to the House Un-
American Activities Committee, agitation for civil rights, growing
opposition to the war in Vietnam—was a decision by the administration to ban student leafleting and advocacy on a part of the campus
known as the Bancroft strip. The strip was university property, although
the university and everyone else assumed it was city property—and the
city had been issuing permits to any students who wanted to use it.
After a call from a newspaper reporter triggered an investigation, the
university realized that its students were on its property engaging in
activities that weren't permitted there—that is, advocating about off-
campus activities. When the school issued a formal ban on such activity, the leftists on campus, including Savio, exploded.

In the demonstrations that followed, Savio emerged as the leading
orator of what we now call the Free Speech Movement.

In every way possible, Pat Brown was unprepared for the unrest at
Berkeley. For one thing, he actually believed in letting students in the
state university system—whose tuition was paid for by the taxpayers—
have free rein politically. He believed that it was a good thing for students to get involved in the issues of the times, including civil rights, the
battle against totalitarianism, and so forth. In a 1961 commencement
speech he gave at Santa Clara University that was widely reported on
and praised—and would come back to be used against him—Brown
said, "Thank God for the spectacle of students picketing—even when
they are picketing me in Sacramento and I think they are wrong—for
students picketing and freedom-riding, for students listening to society's dissidents, for students going into the fields with our migratory
workers, and for marching off to jail with our segregated Negroes. At

last we're getting somewhere. The colleges have become boot camps for citizenship—and citizen-leaders are marching out of them. For a while it will be hard on us administrators. Some students are going to be wrong and some people will deny them the right to make mistakes. Administrators will have to wade through angry letters and colleges will lose some donations. We Governors will have to face indignant caravans and elected officials bent on dictating to state college faculties.

"But let us stand up for our students and be proud of them."

Brown was blindsided when protests at Berkeley turned into something rarely seen in American history: a rebellion that smelled like a revolution. And remember, this was not a rebellion against Republican, conservative administrators. The people in charge at Berkeley were themselves liberals. They never expected the students to turn against them. But that's exactly what happened. And the liberal administrators at Berkeley mishandled the situation badly.

The pot began to boil in September when the activists, many of them, like Savio, newly returned from the South, set up recruiting tables on campus. On October 1, administrators in Sproul Hall approached one of the student leaders, Jack Weinberg, and suggested he take his act elsewhere. As might be expected, Weinberg refused. The administrators then called the police and asked them to remove Weinberg from the plaza. The police arrived in a patrol car.

Thousands of students surrounded the car, with Weinberg inside, handcuffed. The police were trapped in the midst of a threatening crowd. Savio jumped on the car and whipped the protesters into a frenzy.

Then events began to spiral out of control.

Clark Kerr, the University of California's liberal president, met with the activists' leaders and basically caved in to their every demand, promising not to press charges against the demonstrators, and set up a committee to examine the ban on on-campus political activity. In return the students allowed the policemen and their car to go free. It was mob blackmail.

By Thanksgiving, though, as a result of internal politics too complicated to go into in this book, Kerr had a change of heart and announced that he was suspending eight of the leaders of the October demonstration. By now, of course, he had antagonized everybody, from the left-wing students who felt he had broken faith with them to conservatives who thought he had coddled them too much in the first place.

On December 2, 1964, the Berkeley radicals, led by Savio and a few others, held a huge demonstration on campus, and then several hundred of them occupied Sproul Hall. It put Brown in a spot. On the one hand, he was on record as believing that student dissent wasn't a bad thing; on the other, he was horrified that these kids, getting a world-class education on the taxpayers' dime, felt entitled to break the law the way they did. Brown had never gone to college himself (making the leap from high school directly to law school) and he felt that higher education was a gift that shouldn't be snubbed the way these activists were treating it.

Brown tried negotiating at first; he even had a telephone conversation with Mario Savio, arranged by his son Jerry, the future governor; it didn't go well.

Finally, receiving reports that the occupiers were causing property damage and threatening people, he made the decision to get tough. He enlisted Edwin Meese III, the assistant district attorney for Alameda County (and a future attorney general of the United States) and told him, "Take them out of there. Give them every chance to leave and tell them if they don't get out, they'll be arrested."

The police moved in at 3:30 a.m. and began carrying out the occupiers; it took more than three hundred officers twelve hours to remove all the occupiers. That was the end of the occupation; it was also the beginning of the end of Brown's career as governor of California.

The problem for the rest of us was that the free speech the students engaged in was often vicious, hateful, and anti-American. The Free Speech Movement might have started with a deceptively simple request: allow students to participate more in political activities. From there, though, as so often happens, more radical elements took over, and the campus was soon under siege by young people whose very appearance made them seem like hordes of barbarians trying to destroy a carefully built civilization. In the end, of course, one of the greatest accomplishments of the radicals was one they didn't count on; instead of mobilizing the majority in their favor, they created such general revulsion among ordinary folk that their mere presence helped Ronald Reagan, running on a promise to straighten out the situation, become governor in 1966, launching a career that took him to the White House. It was one of the finest examples of the law of unintended consequences working its wonderful, unpredictable magic.

But Berkeley wasn't the only disaster that happened on Brown's watch. His second term was also marked by the race riots in the Watts district of Los Angeles. The violence started with what should have been a routine traffic stop, the kind that happens thousands of times a day all over the country with no further impact, except on the people involved. On the evening of August 11, 1965, a twenty-one-year-old man named Marquette Frye was pulled over on suspicion of driving while intoxicated. Frye was black; the officer who pulled him over was white. Marquette's brother Ronald, who was with him, walked to their nearby house and brought their mother back to the scene. She upbraided Marquette for his drinking—as any good mother would and should, particularly if her son were driving. As she did, however, her son pushed her aside and tried to move toward the crowd that was gathering. As backup police officers tried to arrest him, the crowd grew and began yelling at them and throwing things. Frye's mother and brother were arrested—a tactical mistake. After the Fryes' arrests, the crowd continued to grow, and when additional police tried to break it up they were attacked with rocks and concrete. The police, in an attempt to defuse an ugly situation, began withdrawing from the scene, even as the mob hurled rocks at their cruisers. With the police gone, the crowd continued its depredations, dragging white people from their cars and beating them and attacking random passersby.

Matthew Dallek's *The Right Moment: Ronald Reagan's First Victory and the Decisive Turning Point in American Politics* gives a blow-by-blow of how the police scuffle with the Frye family turned into a confrontation, a confrontation into a riot that left a large part of L.A. smoldering—along with it a large chunk of Pat Brown's political career.

The following day at 2 p.m., a Thursday, the L.A. Human Relations Commission held a meeting in nearby Athens Park. The idea was for Watts residents to air their grievances instead of taking to the streets again that night. They got more than they bargained for—a litany of complaints about joblessness, inadequate housing, and police brutality. Then, a young man took the microphone and lit the fuse with a vengeance. He called for the residents of Watts to go after the white people in their suburbs. "They not going to fight down here no more," he said. "You know where they going? They going after the whites. They going to do the white man in tonight."

Despite official pleas, local TV stations showed clips of this young punk's wild statement. Before the night was over, thousands of angry blacks had taken to the streets, looting, attacking white people, and throwing Molotov cocktails.

L.A.'s police chief at the time was the legendary William H. Parker, a veteran of the invasion of Normandy who had gotten the job in 1950 and went about professionalizing what was universally recognized as an out-of-shape, corrupt, and overmanned police force. Among other accomplishments, he had been the first big city chief to integrate his force. Not that that was doing him any good as Watts went up in flames.

Parker quickly realized that, as battle-ready and well-trained as his men were, he simply didn't have enough of them to contain the carnage in Watts. He did what any leader would do in a similar situation—he called for reinforcements, in this case the National Guard, which was under the command of the governor. It should have been a simple matter—one phone call to bring overwhelming force to bear on the malefactors in Watts and bring peace back to L.A.

Parker made his phone call.

Then he waited.

And waited.

The problem was that Brown had the bad luck to be traveling in the Mediterranean—I think he was in Greece—when the riots broke out, the worst possible situation for an elected official to be in when a crisis erupts. And this was in the era before innovations like e-mail and Skype made the world a much smaller place. Although he could (and did) check in by phone during his return to the United States, Brown was not properly in place in his command center—the governor's mansion—and he couldn't properly assess the situation.

In his place in Sacramento stood Lieutenant Governor Glenn Anderson. And Anderson had his eye on a different crisis, the one that was bubbling away up north in Berkeley.

Earlier in the day, Anderson had been assured that the violence that had flared up on Wednesday was well in hand. But that came before the peace conference in Athens Park and the incendiary news clips that triggered a far worse cataclysm.

He had also been told that student radicals at Berkeley were planning major protests for Friday—including blocking a troop train filled with GIs heading to Vietnam. With L.A. under control, as he thought, he felt his place was at a meeting of the University of California Regents in Berkeley.

He made the wrong choice, but he didn't yet know it. When a commission later investigated the Watts riots, Anderson had this to say: "I had been told at 7 o'clock [in the morning] that the riots had been contained, they weren't going to need the Guard." Then he said, rather ruefully, "I could have stayed in Los Angeles and something could have broken out up [north] and they could have said, 'How come you weren't up in Berkeley where all this thing was going to happen and you were told so in all of the morning papers?'"

The riots began around 9:15 a.m. shortly after Anderson took off for Berkeley. Parker made his call for help around 11:00. What followed was a day of delay and prevarication and poor leadership by Anderson, much of it caused by bad advice from Brown's advisers.

It seemed to everyone—not just those of us on the Right—that all of California's young people were in rebellion against the legitimate authority of law, parents, church—any form of meaningful tradition. Under Brown's inept leadership, the state government appeared helpless, so much so that its inaction made it seem like an accomplice in its own looming demise. When he should have been working to defuse the violence, Pat Brown looked like an enabler of the protests, a weak and permissive Democrat patsy; a big-spending, big government, big-D Democrat.

The immediate result of all this was that Sam Yorty, the mayor of Los Angeles, decided to challenge Brown, mounting an attack from the right of the Democratic Party.

Yorty was an interesting character, saddled all his life with the title of "maverick." A fiery scrapper who believed in the New Deal and the rights of the working man, he had first been elected to the State Legislature in 1936. He was so identified as a left-winger at the time that he was one of the state Democrats linked to the Communist Party in a 1938 article in the *L.A. Times.* Yorty's trip rightward was head-snappingly fast, much faster than Ronald Reagan's. By 1939 he had turned against the Left completely. "Communists are rats!" he said at a legislative committee hearing, "a bunch of rats!"

Elected mayor of L.A. in 1961, Yorty nourished his feuds, and the one with Pat Brown went back decades. For one thing, Yorty, a World War II combat veteran, resented that Brown hadn't served in the war. "He got his start in politics while the rest of us went into military service," he railed. Yorty despised Brown so much that in 1962, when Brown ran against Nixon, Yorty didn't endorse him.

So that was the Democratic primary: a mainstream, liberal establishment figure running against a more right-wing, law-and-order insurgent. By odd coincidence, a similar dynamic was about to play out on the Republican side.

When Brown announced that he planned to run for reelection in '66, breaking his promise not to seek a third term, he presented California's Republicans with the fight they wanted. He was already weakened by the chaos of the times. He was no longer the Pat Brown who had defeated Knowland and destroyed Richard Nixon. He could be beaten, if he made it past Yorty, by the right candidate. The Old Guard Republicans looked at the changed political landscape and took heart.

Here, they thought, was an opportunity to return to Sacramento in triumph.

The obvious candidate to unseat Pat Brown—at least as far as the northern GOP Establishment saw it—was George Christopher, the fifty-eight-year-old mayor of San Francisco.

Those of the southern part of the state weren't convinced. Christopher was that thing we couldn't abide—a moderate Republican, and he was from the unreliable North. His big claim to fame was that he had brought the New York Giants baseball team to San Francisco in 1958. He also managed to get the funding to build Candlestick Park, home for the newly rechristened San Francisco Giants. Even if we were baseball fans in Southern California—although more likely to be Los Angeles Dodgers fans—that just wasn't enough to sway us.

Christopher had been born in Greece, and moved with his family to San Francisco in 1910. He left school at fourteen, sold newspapers, talked his way into a job as a copy boy at the *San Francisco Examiner*, and studied accounting in night school. Later he started a successful dairy and eventually decided to try his hand at politics, becoming mayor of San Francisco in 1955. He made a name for himself by backing civil rights, clearing slums, and building schools, always under accusations that his ambitious programs were fiscally unsound. He was, we realized, just another big-spending politician in Republican clothing.

And he did something that truly infuriated those of us who felt the Cold War against the Soviet Union was the most important fight in the world now that World War II was over, hosting Soviet boss Nikita Khrushchev on a 1959 tour of America. Then he compounded the offense by visiting Khrushchev in Moscow the next year.

Still, to the Establishment, Christopher was a safe choice, and it was, in the grander scheme of things, his turn to advance.

But he had one additional drawback that bothered the Young Turks almost as much as his ideological squishiness—he had no personality. None. Not to slander all accountants, but his chosen profession had left its mark on him. He was dull, dull, dull. He couldn't light up a room. He couldn't dazzle anyone with his wit because he had none. He was solid and reliable, but so was every accountant worth his salt. And he wasn't running for controller, he was running for governor against an incumbent who despite his flaws was a natural retail politician.

For the Young Turks, living in the shadow of Hollywood, where charisma flowed like tap water (from the north, ironically, I realize), Christopher's lack of sparkle proved unforgivable. They wanted a different candidate, a candidate with personality, a candidate with a pulse, a candidate with star power. They wanted a candidate who could end Pat Brown's career.

Still the party elders backed Christopher despite the widespread doubts—in both wings of the party—that such a snooze-inducing man could beat Brown even in the governor's weakened state and allowing for his penchant for making self-destructive gaffes.

Christopher might be running, and he might have powerful backers, but there was another candidate, just waiting in the wings, waiting for the call. At least that's what Holmes Tuttle, one of the most powerful voices in Southern California commerce, thought. He had his candidate ready.

Tuttle considered himself a very fine judge of character. After all, that's how he got rich. He could take the true measure of the people around him, test for weakness, assess the strengths, seal the deal. He knew who could stand the fire and who would break under pressure. A tall, quiet man of true grit, Tuttle had fought, clawed, and charmed his own way to the top. That's how he learned the secrets of spotting a winner.

Born in Oklahoma in 1905, Tuttle was only seventeen when his father died. It was a transformative moment, but he knew that his future lay somewhere else. He decided to ride the rails, looking for greener pastures. It wasn't an uncommon route in those early days of adventure-seeking American entrepreneurs. Tuttle, like many of those unsettled souls, went from job to job, searching for his proper place in the world, which he felt certain lay high up in the commercial wind. Nor did he waste his time. He took jobs that led somewhere; he picked up experience and a kind of savvy from every task. The payoff came when he worked on a Ford assembly line and learned everything there was to know about cars.

That brought him to California and a job in a car dealership. Through the force of his bighearted personality and self-starting drive, he soon had his own Ford dealership. There are some men—impressive personalities—who can make you see the sunny side to a simple transaction, like buying a car. That was Holmes Tuttle. Still a young man, he owned one car dealership, then got another. By the time he was sixty, he owned scores of Ford dealerships throughout the Southwest. To this day, there's a Holmes Tuttle Ford dealership in Tucson, Arizona, although it's doubtful if many people seeing the sign realize the historical importance of the man for whom it's named.

Two months after Goldwater's campaign went down in flames, Tuttle gathered a meeting of his friends in Palm Springs. Among them: William French Smith, Reagan's attorney and a future attorney general of the United States; Henry Salvatori, founder of the Western Geophysical Co. (more about him later); and Taft Schneider, an executive at MCA who had convinced Reagan to make the switch to the small screen. Tuttle's opinion carried weight with these substantial men of commerce of southern California. And now he was telling them about his candidate, a man, he said, who had the right view of the world combined with outsize gifts of personality and glamour, a candidate who would light up the California sky and incinerate Pat Brown. That man was Ronald Reagan.

That meeting heralded the start of the Friends of Ronald Reagan, the stalwarts who would follow him all the way. They had several characteristics in common—an unswerving belief in the free market; a bred-in-the-bone hatred of Communism, coupled with a distrust of the liberals who they thought enabled its insidious progress in America; and a belief that Ronald Reagan was the eloquent spokesman who could carry their message to the country.

The proposal that Reagan run for governor of California, however, came as a mild shock even to Reagan's staunchest friends. "No, no. Jimmy Stewart for governor, Ronald Reagan for best friend," movie mogul Jack Warner said when he heard of the proposed Reagan candidacy. It was one of those utterances repeated and reported all across Hollywood—Reagan even good-naturedly told it on himself—because it had such a ring of accurately capturing the studio mindset at the time. But people like Warner missed the point. If Reagan wasn't a darkly smoldering leading man, he had an ineffable appeal that went deeper than that of a mere matinee idol. He had an uncomplicated, friendly quality that people responded to. That was what had made him so good at the best-buddy roles that he played. And it would be solid gold when he asked people for their votes.

Anyone who spent any time around Reagan knew that he had the opinions and instincts of a true politician. "If that son of a bitch doesn't stop making speeches, he'll end up in the White House," said Alan Hale (as quoted in Edmund Morris's idiosyncratic *Dutch*).

There was also this: It seemed there was nothing devious or dangerous about Reagan. Even his humor had a kind of homespun, corny goodwill, rather like another underrated Republican politician from Illinois, Abraham Lincoln. Here was a man you could trust.

Holmes Tuttle trusted him. He trusted him even though Reagan had started out as a true-believer New Deal Democrat and Tuttle was a solid Republican, an Eisenhower man. But men, as Tuttle knew, came to California to change their lives, to start over. They changed professions, changed their names, their wives, and their hair color. Who was to say a man couldn't change his political philosophy?

Tuttle had first met Reagan in 1946. Just out of the Army, Dutch needed a new car, and he bought it from Tuttle. They impressed each other so much that Tuttle spent the next two decades trying to sell Reagan on the idea of becoming a Republican and running for public office.

6

Stealth Campaign

I didn't know it at the time, but when I went to hear Reagan speak in that little schoolroom, he was already in the race. Nothing formal, mind you. Nothing definite. No hint that he was going to declare officially. He was being very coy. Very carefully, very delicately, he was dipping his toe into the political waters, testing them.

Did people really want him to run? Did they really like him enough to vote for him? Did his philosophy—unabashedly patriotic in a time of widespread dissent, uncompromisingly conservative just after the conservative standard-bearer Goldwater had been routed—make their hearts beat faster? He went all around the state, testing, testing, testing. Everywhere he went, however large the crowd was or however small, there were people like me, people who felt the country was headed in the wrong direction, our state leading the way. Some of us asked him if he was planning to run for governor. Some of us went beyond asking and begged him, please, to run.

The stars were aligning for the transformation of Ronald Reagan. His years as GE's spokesman, traveling the country to address the company's workers, had laid the foundation for a constituency that would only grow greater, the nucleus of the so-called Reagan Democrats we would hear so much about a few years later. "By 1958, according to

TV Guide," says *Ronnie and Nancy*, "he had visited more than 130 GE factories in twenty-five states and met nearly 200,000 workers."

It was grueling work—Reagan hated to fly, so he traveled everywhere either by train or car—and he wrote tender letters to Nancy, telling her how lonely it was on the road. But there were benefits to his solitude—plenty of time in empty hotel rooms to read books and digest the political philosophy that he was now expounding in front of rapt audiences.

And as he traveled, The Speech mutated, becoming stronger, more passionate. Reagan was working on it like a sculptor working on a piece of art.

When he wasn't touring the GE plants, he was on his ranch, riding his horses, enjoying the outdoor California life. When he wasn't on the ranch, he and Nancy were socializing with the likes of Alfred and Betsy Bloomingdale, Walter and Lee Annenberg, the Robert Taylors, Edgar and Frances Bergen (she a former high fashion model and the leader of a strong faction of Hollywood society), James and Gloria Stewart, Dick Powell and wife June Allyson, William Holden and wife Brenda Marshall. All friends. All powerful. All wealthy. All ready to help when the time came.

The GE connection opened other doors. Reagan delivered The Speech to the National Association of Manufacturers, to executive clubs of all the major cities, to chambers of commerce around the country. And he continued to hammer his great theme, as recorded in Bob Colacello's book: "I went out of my way to point out the problems of centralizing power in Washington."

Before, in the early Fifties, when Reagan retired as president of the Screen Actor's Guild, Tuttle had asked him to run for the US Senate, but he'd turned him down. "I'd like to keep making horse operas. I'm a ham—always was, always will be," he said, Tuttle recalled in an oral history.

But that wasn't to be. Universal had cut his contract from five pictures to three; then GE fired him. But the truly seismic change came on October 27, 1964, when he made the Goldwater speech and stole the show. After the Goldwater presidential debacle, after the endless postmortems about how and why the wheels came off, Tuttle, the upbeat morale officer of the group, told a meeting of the highest power brokers: "We don't want this to be the demise of the Republican Party."

Bill Roberts (more about him shortly) recalled that Tuttle saved the party hierarchy from falling into a funk at that meeting. They had not only endured the Goldwater bruising, but they were still smarting from Pat Brown's defeat of Nixon in 1962.

The party desperately needed an unambiguous win. The most passionate conservatives were beginning to get the feeling that they might have missed the tide of history. When Eisenhower took office in 1952, some of the true believers had expected that he'd dismantle the whole abominable New Deal down to the last Social Security dime. Of course, that wasn't a realistic expectation, and it didn't happen. Then Nixon had fallen to Kennedy in 1960.

But there were more pragmatic conservatives in the ranks. Late in 1965, at one of those political autopsies with oil baron Henry Salvatori, Tuttle made his pitch. He had the perfect guy waiting in the wings, he said. His name was Ronald Reagan. He could revive the Republican Party, Tuttle said. He could send Pat Brown scurrying out of Sacramento in 1966.

They were ideal partners, Tuttle and Salvatori. Tuttle was the son of a Main Street, Chamber of Commerce, Establishment Republican. He had worked for Eisenhower, but he still harbored a warm spot in his heart for hotheaded uncompromising conservatives like Salvatori.

Henry Salvatori was born in Italy in 1901, and his mother carried him to America in her arms. Salvatori became a proud, unapologetic, full-throated American patriot. His father had a small farm, but

Salvatori had larger goals. He worked his way through the University of Pennsylvania where he earned a degree in electrical engineering. With a scholarship from Bell Telephone Laboratories, he went to Columbia University where he earned a master's degree in physics. Then Salvatori went out into the oil fields of Oklahoma and developed seismic methods for finding oil. He started his own oil exploration company and became rich. Along the way, he also became an ardent anti-Communist, a strong supporter of civil rights, and a true conservative.

He and Holmes Tuttle had earned the right to call themselves self-made men.

If there was one reason that Reagan made for the ideal choice for both men, it was that they were both convinced that he would unite the party. California Republicans had split so badly that George Christopher, win or lose, would only solidify the preexisting divisions. But Ronald Reagan—with his folksy ambiguity and his lopsided winning smile—would never make anyone mad. Everyone could get behind him.

But there was something else, at least for some of them—something that they would never publicly admit—a slightly dismissive contempt for the intellectual basis of his beliefs. Reagan might say all the right things and stand with them on important issues, but he was, at bottom, a lot of them thought, merely an actor playing a part.

Tuttle pushed his position, the skeptics be damned. If Tuttle was the conciliator, Salvatori was the inquisitor. Fine, he liked Reagan—everyone liked Reagan—but how to go about it?

7

The Candidate

First they had to convince Reagan that he was running. He knew it, of course, but there were problems, and like a barefoot man certain there are tacks on the carpet, he was reluctant to take that first big step into the darkness.

Hollywood gave him the push that he needed, but not in the way that you might expect. His acting career was finished; the 1964 film, *The Killers,* was a critical and financial flop. It was his last major role.

Finally, he knew; he was fifty-five years old and no longer star-struck. Nevertheless, as Reagan continued to insist, when pressed by Tuttle, he couldn't run for anything without financial security; he had to feed his family. By now, he and Nancy had two children, Patti, born in 1952, and Ron, born in 1958. He had a house in Pacific Palisades and a ranch in Malibu Canyon. In 1951, he bought 290 acres for $85,000—$293 an acre. It turned out to be a great investment, and 20th Century-Fox often used the land as locations for its Westerns. In 1965, a group of Reagan's Hollywood supporters (including Darryl Zanuck) got Fox to buy 236 acres for $1.9 million, or $8,178 an acre—a 2,500 percent profit. It solved Reagan's financial worries.

Now he could turn full-blast to politics.

Other factors came into play as well, though. Reagan wanted to be certain that he wouldn't be ridiculed—which, of course, no one could absolutely guarantee. He told Tuttle and Salvatori that he wanted to tour the state. Make small appearances, gauge the enthusiasm.

"You are going to have to fly," Salvatori told him, according to Bill Roberts. "It's a big state."

Reagan replied with one of those evasive, resigned shrugs that meant that he would do what he had to do, even if it meant flying. "There's lots of trains," Roberts remembered him saying.

In February 1965, Ronald Reagan—having heard from the kitchen cabinet, not to mention Arlene Dahl's tea leaf prediction to Nancy that he would be governor—was leaning.

Tuttle's first move was to hire professionals to manage Reagan's campaign. "We checked with people around the country, and they said Spencer-Roberts was the best," he told Lou Cannon. "We didn't want anything less than the best."

So he called Stuart Spencer, then in his late thirties. Spencer had emerged from the Navy in 1946 and gone into coaching and athletics, but all of his friends were coming out of the service, and, it seemed, all were running for public office. They asked Spencer for help. Famous as a level-headed tactical genius, he was very good at managing political campaigns—a natural. Of forty congressional races, thirty-four of his candidates won.

Spencer and Bill Roberts had only been in business as Spencer-Roberts Consultants since 1960, but they had become the gold standard for campaign management. They managed Nelson Rockefeller's presidential bid in 1964, and although it failed the political pros acknowledged that they had handled it with savvy and skill. In fact, the Goldwater people told Tuttle that they still carried bruises from going up against Spencer-Roberts. Imagine what they'd do to George Christopher and, when his turn came, Pat Brown.

The only trouble was that George Christopher wanted to hire Spencer-Roberts as well. In truth, Spencer and Roberts had reservations about both Republican candidates. Christopher had lost twice in statewide races, so he had that slight whiff of failure clinging to him. He was also mayor of San Francisco, which wouldn't play very well in southern California. "We wrestled with it," Spencer said (in Cannon's book). "George was the favorite, he was the favorite of the party, the polls, the media, everything. But when push came to shove, we didn't think there was any growth for Christopher."

And Reagan? They were concerned that he was too right wing and that he would simply crash and burn the same way Goldwater had. They had also been warned, among other things, that he was an insubstantial crackpot, a prima donna, a martinet impossible to work with—a whole host of reasons that made them hesitate about taking him on.

So Spencer spent time talking to Christopher, and he spent time talking to Reagan, and in the end he picked Reagan because he liked his sense of humor.

The red socks won them over. When they visited his home, Reagan crossed his legs and revealed a pair of blazing red socks. It was, he said, his Commie footwear. If he could joke about something like that, he was definitely their kind of guy.

If Spencer and Roberts were professional political operatives, Tuttle was the rainmaker. He made things happen. He laid it out to the Friends of Ronald Reagan: There was no one else, he told them. Christopher could never win over anyone from Orange County, the hardcore Republicans. His blandness might drive away moderates. Only Reagan could patch the divide.

They officially named themselves the Friends of Ronald Reagan, and among their number they also counted insurance executive Asa Call, the brains behind the resurgence of Richard Nixon; Texas oilman Jack Wrather; William Randolph Hearst Jr.; Walt Disney; and then the movie stars: Jimmy Cagney, William Holden, John Wayne, Robert Taylor . . . and, as the billboards used to say, many, many more.

That was the great thing about Hollywood then: You could be a fading B-movie actor yet still count the great stars as your friends. Reagan had a knack for making and keeping friends. He sat at the Jewish table at the Warner Bros. commissary, among other reasons, to pick up jokes to weave into his endless speaking appearances. He lived within close range of Dick Powell and June Allyson; he was friends with Jimmy Stewart; and he brushed up against all of the major players at the nonstop barbecues and dinner parties in the art colony of Hollywood Hills.

And he was passionate about his politics.

Earlier it had been one thing. "He's a boring liberal," the actress Marsha Hunt, herself an ultra-liberal, told gossip columnists about his days as SAG president. "He would buttonhole you at a party and talk liberalism at you. You'd look for an escape."

Now he was a conservative, but he didn't change his performance. It didn't seem to matter which side he came down on, Reagan liked to hold forth. A famous anecdote repeated in all of the Reagan biographies concerns a dinner party at Jack Benny's house. When Reagan kept going on and on about the intrusion of government and the unfairness of the tax code, Jack, already calling him "Governor," said, "Oh, c'mon, Ronnie, sit down and finish your dinner."

The first thing that they had to do was put together an exploratory committee. Make arrangements for him to meet people—little speeches in front of the Elks or a Chamber of Commerce, or any gathering of Californians. He would see how it went over, how they liked him, if he still had the old charm. Then he would decide. The final answer wasn't necessary until January 1966. Even Roberts and Spencer were cagey, having to do their own due diligence by putting the candidate through the wringer—a kind of political audition.

It could be done, of course. Helen Gahagan Douglas, whatever else you might think or say about her, had been in show biz (her only big-screen credit was in *She*, the film adaptation of H. Rider Haggard's rip-roaring nineteenth-century adventure story and immortal source of the line "She Who Must Be Obeyed") before she was elected to Congress. George Murphy, the old song-and-dance man turned actor was elected to the US Senate in 1964. That meant an actor could be taken seriously by the electorate. There were precedents. But Murphy was a savvy politician. He'd had a full show business career, from playing musical stars (*For Me and My Gal*, 1942) to sympathetic soldiers (*Battleground*, 1949). Much like Reagan, he earned accolades by handling the business end of the business of show for his peers. He served as president of the Screen Actors Guild from 1944 to 1946. He arranged the entertainment for Eisenhower's inauguration.

At the time, "We didn't know Reagan," Stu Spencer said an oral history, "and Reagan didn't know us. But Holmes knew us all. George Murphy, who never gets mentioned, was the bridge. George used to sit me down and say, 'I've got to tell you about Ronnie. He's stubborn. He's this. He's that.' And all the time he was laughing because he really liked Ronnie a lot and respected his enthusiasm."

Spencer worried in particular about Reagan's potential support from people who belonged to the John Birch Society, which opposed American membership in the United Nations and believed that liberals were intent on creating a "one-world socialist government in the United States." A retired candy baron named Robert Welch Jr. and a group of like-minded souls named their organization after John Birch, an intelligence officer shot in China just after the end of World War II, claiming him as the first American to die in what soon became known as the Cold War. The Birchers opposed most government programs and were hostile to civil rights enforcement by the federal government.

Spencer was especially sensitive about the subject after running the campaign of John Rousselot, an insurance agent who won a seat in Congress from Southern California in '64. When Spencer asked Rousselot if he was a member of the Birch society, Rousselot denied it. But on a plane ride after the election, he admitted that he was a member.

Rousselot went on to have a checkered career in Congress, winning and losing seats in gerrymandered districts.

But the fact was, in the mid '60s, membership in the John Birch Society had become a kiss of death for any candidate seeking statewide office. Any hint of Bircher approval drove away more moderate voters (both Republican and Democrat) in droves; even Goldwater had suffered from their endorsement.

Reagan denied any direct link to the Birchers, but people with Birch sympathies supported him; after all, he was the most conservative candidate, even if he didn't endorse their more extreme positions. Reagan accepted that support with the same rationale that Goldwater had used: They were coming over to his side, not vice versa.

If Spencer and Roberts were extra cautious, it was understandable. After all, they still had dealings with Nelson Rockefeller, still counted on his support, still considered themselves moderates. When Rockefeller was running for president in '64, Spencer approached him and said that they needed help from the Eastern Republican Establishment. Rockefeller laughed and shook his head and said, "You're looking at the Eastern Republican Establishment," Spencer recalled.

Young and eager, Spencer and Roberts warmed to Reagan. First came the red socks, then the allure of taking on a long shot to beat the odds. Meanwhile Tuttle and Salvatori's emerging organization was willing to roll the dice. In the early summer of 1965, the Friends of Ronald Reagan sent out a letter to Republican activists entitled "A Time for Choosing":

"For several years, Ronald Reagan has spoken out forcefully and eloquently to the above subject. Again and again, he has called upon the American public to awaken to a decision they must ultimately make. Simply put, the question was, and still is: Will the people control the government or will the government control the people? . . . Ronald Reagan, out of a deep sense of duty and dedication, is willing to serve his Republican Party as its candidate for governor providing a substantial cross-section of our Party will unite behind his candidacy."

More than forty names graced the letter, all major players in California Republican politics. The response affirmed Reagan's appeal. More than $135,000 rolled in just to fund the exploratory stage of the campaign—more than enough to get the ball rolling. Everyone agreed that there had to be a trial run. Reagan wouldn't publicly declare unless the people—the real people, not just the big shots in Palm Springs—wanted him.

So Nancy packed peanut butter sandwiches, and they hired a driver and sent Reagan touring California, which is 750 miles long from Crescent City to Chula Vista, as the crow flies, and some 250 miles wide, with lots of highs and lows: from Death Valley's 282-foot drop below sea level to Mt. Whitney at 14,494 feet high.

In the driver's seat of the car sat Bill Friedman, a retired Los Angeles police sergeant, a solid man over six feet tall, no stranger to celebrity security. Friedman had taken care of Errol Flynn from time to time and told stories of how the dashing actor drank himself half crazy, becoming a character from one of his swashbuckling films. Once, Flynn playfully wrestled Friedman's gun away at a party and had to be talked down by the good-natured ex-cop. Reagan himself was no physical slouch, six-foot-one and 170 pounds. He kept in shape by swimming and riding horses, but for now he tucked himself into the back seat of the car and went through the stops on Route 405 like the good sport that he was. They deliberately avoided the big cities—San

Diego, Los Angeles, San Francisco. They didn't want the reporters to get their teeth into him. It was a small-town tour, an out-of-town tryout: American Legion outposts, library meetings, schoolroom lectures. As they went up and down the state, Reagan developed more confidence.

Stu Spencer, as he remembered, saw him develop firsthand: "He was shy. The first time we took him to West Covina (I remember the town), I took him to somebody's house to a fund-raiser. They probably had fifty to seventy-five people there. He walked in with Nancy. He goes over to the corner of the room and stands there. The people are milling around here, and the bar is over there. I'm watching all this. Finally I walked over to him and I said, 'Ron, you've got to get out there and mix. You've got to rub shoulders.'

"He was used to people coming to him. I said, 'You've got to go press the hands. You've got to move it.'

"He didn't like doing that. No, he didn't like doing that. Not that he was all above that. He was a shy person and didn't want to walk up to you and say, 'I'm Ronald Reagan, and I'm running for governor.'

"Now the exact opposite to that was Nelson Rockefeller. He'd work the room if there were three people in it. It was always, 'Hiya, fella, Hiya, fella.'

"Just the opposite type of person (Reagan). At communications, one on one, he was not very good. At global communications, the stage, he was fabulous."

Reagan kept fending off questions about his official status. "By January—I'll make a decision by January." But during that summer, Spencer and Roberts knew. One day Spencer looked at Roberts and said, "This guy's running. To hell with the exploratory stuff, he's made up his mind."

8

The Blunder

"To compel a man to furnish contributions of money for the propagation of opinions which he disbelieves is sinful and tyrannical."
—THOMAS JEFFERSON, FROM A COLLECTION OF
INSPIRATIONAL QUOTATIONS KEPT BY RONALD REAGAN

Throughout history—from Spartacus to Thomas Paine—angry, aggrieved citizens have cried out against the king's oppressive writ. By now, Ronald Reagan, citizen-orator, was fed up with his own political environment. He'd been to the mountains of California, and he'd been to the valleys; he'd been to the farms, and he'd been to the public square where he talked to the people. Finally, he was ready to raise his own voice against the prevailing political writ.

The last time that he spoke out in full throat was when he recently switched parties, officially becoming a Republican. It was the speech he made for Barry Goldwater in 1964; he had appeared in front of a friendly crowd in a big auditorium. But for this particular announcement he didn't want a big auditorium or even a big audience. With his uncanny instinct for staging and command, he wanted the statement to be intimate. Just him and the camera—they always got along.

Then came the swarm of advisers, consultants, and spinners, buzzing in his ears: Sure, "A Time for Choosing" is a great speech, but this isn't a national audience. This is about California. Remember, you're not running for president; you're running for *governor*.

In his book *The Education of Ronald Reagan*, Thomas W. Evans puts it this way: "Most candidates evolve from the local to the national stage. Reagan reversed the process.... As he admitted privately, he had devoted so much time to 'overall philosophy, national and international policy, that [he] did not know anything about the organization of state government, the problems and what would be the issues in state government.'"

He was a big-picture guy, and the race for the nomination was a small-picture (or at least smaller-picture race). The last two Republicans to take on Pat Brown had been doomed by the perception that their sights were set on Washington, D.C., not Sacramento.

Therefore, the advisers, consultants, and spinners "helped him out." Not that he stood for a lot of help. Reagan liked to freckle his speeches with his words—words that felt familiar and homegrown—and that always made him seem more authentic. Indeed, it made him more authentic. That was the trick. The man summoned up his own instinctive feelings about things, and it came forth in his own words.

Still, he had his advisers, and he took what he wanted from the boys, made some adjustments, fashioned what he thought was a pretty good twenty-nine-minute speech.

On Tuesday, January 4, 1966, after the Tuttles and Salvatoris put up the money for half an hour on prime-time television and hired a professional announcer to introduce him, Reagan walked across the den of his home in Pacific Palisades and—in his folksy, homespun manner—told the people of California that he was ready to take back the state.

He stood impressively before a burning fireplace, sporting an informal jacket with the edge of a handkerchief showing from the breast pocket, wearing a regimental necktie and a smile not too bright and not too grim (it was a serious, man-of-the-people smile). He had been very careful about making this decision, he told the television audience. He had spent six months crisscrossing the state by plane, train, and automobile, talking to a cross-section of its citizens. He had thrown a snowball in the morning and watched people water-ski in the afternoon, and he had, in his travels over the nation-sized state, heard the true voice of the people.

For dramatic effect, he picked up a thick report from his desk—it was the product of all the commissions on California's state government; in that simple gesture, he identified the crux of the matter. If there was no way to count the number of boards and commissions operating in the state, then state government was spinning out of control. Still holding the prop, he cleverly leaned against his desk as if the weight of this revelation were almost unbearable. There was no way to teach or coach such a move; only a convinced public artist would sense the right step to clarify, to make visible, what he was saying.

As he moved around the den and switched from topic to topic, he laid out the Republican case. On the issue of civil rights, he was unimpeachably against discrimination. There was no excuse for being unfair to citizens of a different color or creed. However, he added, he "seriously questioned" whether anything further was needed by government to promote that fairness. People, he insisted, had to act on the Golden Rule.

Some insisted later that this statement attacked the Civil Rights Act of 1964. It was the Southern states' argument for handling civil rights locally, that the federal government shouldn't meddle with the natural, evolutionary death of discrimination. In other words, you can't legislate a change of heart. For Reagan, this belief held constant with his call for limited government. But his position came back to haunt him in the form of a blindsided attack on his integrity and evenhandedness when it came to race.

As Reagan spoke about conditions in the state, a crisp impatience crept into his tone. He made a quiet show of subdued temper, as if he had been holding back his anger—not blaming anyone, just stepping in before it was too late, trying to get it right.

Government, he declared, was supposed to grow along with the population of a state. Keep a rational balance between need and income. But California government was growing four times faster than the population, and the state politicians in Washington were seeking to increase California's debt, which fell to each family of four to the tune of $1,396. The political leaders wanted $200 million in new taxes, $260 million to build new schools, and another $250 million to create make-work jobs.

That's not what the situation called for, he said. The state needed less social tinkering and more laws to strengthen the police. He attacked the elimination of residency requirements for state aid and said working people shouldn't have to provide assistance for people who viewed welfare as a way of life.

Then, to bolster his argument, he pulled out the numbers. After World War II, he said, two of every hundred Californians collected welfare. The number had now grown to more than fifteen of one hundred; 15.1 percent, to be exact.

From a deeply felt Republican stance at the core of his rebuilt beliefs, he delivered his attack on swollen bureaucracy and federal interference with confident determination.

"Look at us. Can you believe that anyone can manage our lives better than ourselves?"

Some twenty-five minutes into the prime-time speech, he formally and publicly declared his candidacy for governor.

At first the speech was well received, its delivery judged smooth and polished. The content was familiar, expected, the usual litany of Republican battle cries and complaints about big government, Big

Brother, big taxes—the heavy burden of the undeserving poor borne by the hard-working earners.

But there had been a glitch.

Reagan had taken his stand and outlined his positions with conviction. He bolstered his case with mathematical precision, statistics even, while holding in his hand a report on state commissions. It was all so unassailable. Naturally, reporters would check his claims, match his facts against the record, but in those pre-Internet days it took a few hours before anyone realized the size of the catastrophe.

Reagan had given the number of California residents on welfare at more than 15 percent. It struck everyone as high; it even justified a significant level of outrage. However, when reporters fact-checked the numbers, they discovered his mistake. The correct figure wasn't 15.1 percent—it was 5.1 percent. In a single breath, he had tripled the number of welfare recipients. Someone had made a typographical error in the speech—and it was a whopper.

But it wasn't just the mix-up of digits that was disturbing; anyone could confuse a few numbers. That wasn't the heart of the blunder. The numerical slip unwittingly proved the chief underlying complaint against Reagan: that he was merely reciting words and numbers from a script. He didn't really understand the situation. A real politician would have known the difference, out in the world, between 5 percent and 15. He lacked gravitas. Critics and skeptics could thus dismiss him as a failed actor trying to save a doomed career by leaping into high political office by misrepresenting the truth. The governor's office of the nation's most populous state (as of 1962, almost twenty million souls) was no place for an amateur, a dilettante with no real experience in handling the grand wheel of state. This was, in short, no way to launch a political career.

Not all of those critics were Democrats.

The staff at Spencer-Roberts had long had concerns about Reagan's substance. There was no doubt that he had the charismatic gifts;

he could always connect with his audience. The people liked him, especially women. But he didn't seem to grasp the full scope or nature of state politics. He didn't even seem to care much about the subject, and he frequently scrambled figures, like the welfare statistics. Worst of all, though, whenever he faced the press, he tended to deliver long, rambling answers to simple questions.

So far it had been a small problem. Reporters who met Reagan at those informal press conferences tended to cut him some slack. It was condescending—lowering the bar for a B-movie actor going in over his head—but slack nonetheless. As the *San Francisco Chronicle* put it: "Let us agree that if Mr. Reagan's gallant performance as an amateur politician who decides to run for governor remains unconvincing . . . it was simply a flagrant example of miscasting."

The bemused eye-rolling and off-center forgiveness signaled that they didn't take him too seriously. Implicit was the conviction that the recycled actor would eventually give way to the more experienced George Christopher.

Reagan's backers understandably took alarm. They immediately summoned a reliable old fireman, Lyn Nofziger, for help. Even at forty-two he was a perpetually hangdog middle-aged man, a cigar dangling from his lips, a Mickey Mouse tie flying at half-mast from his rumpled shirt, a look of amused scorn floating from his face. A native of Bakersfield, Nofziger had attended San Jose City College where he quickly became a Republican, albeit one with a wicked sense of humor. He served in the Army and went to work as a reporter in the Copley newspaper chain's Washington bureau, bumping up against all the political operatives aswarm there. Soon recognized as a friendly and capable man, he was recruited to work for Reagan late in '65. Still, the newspaperman in him always lingered, and he carried his manual typewriter wherever he went. Stuart Spencer described him as "profane, disheveled, and always quick with a quip."

There's a great story about how Nofziger and Reagan met, at a cocktail party in Columbus, Ohio, earlier in 1965. It was Nofziger's birthday, and he began celebrating early. By the time Reagan showed up late, Nofziger was, as they say, half in the bag. Undeterred by his enfeebled condition, Nofziger approached Reagan and introduced himself. Nofziger asked him a few journalistic questions about his rumored candidacy, took notes, then stumbled off into the night, feeling the weight of Reagan's disapproval.

Two months later, Nofziger called Reagan's brother, Neil, an acquaintance, and set up a lunch where he could, sober this time, interview Reagan. They met at the Brown Derby in Hollywood.

"You may not remember, but we've met before," Nofziger said to Reagan.

Reagan looked back at him straight-faced and replied: "Yes, I do."

It was a bad start, but Nofziger recovered from it, and it was that unshaven throwback to the *Front Page* era of journalism who was hired to help save Reagan. He might have been big and sloppy, but he always had an answer, and it was always a grown-up solution to a crisis. Nofziger provided a sobering presence—and the adjective is definitely ironic—in the chaos of passionate causes. And Reagan liked him. That was always an asset.

But the real problem wasn't one of surface appeal or even an adjustment in tone. The candidate himself had a serious flaw, one that could allow George Christopher to make swift work of him in the looming Republican primary. He lacked an intimate knowledge of the working of state government: the way the State Legislature functioned, the method of passing laws, the role of the governor in all this. All that in addition to the burden of learning and mastering the art of being a candidate.

Ronald Reagan had to go back to school.

At first they brought in Charles J. Conrad, a fifty-eight-year-old former bit actor—thinking that a connection would form naturally

Reagan and Nofziger in the foreground looking off to the left (background figures unknown).

with an old colleague. Conrad had appeared in a few *Perry Mason* episodes and had served as an assemblyman, so they had that in common: acting and politics. The two men had several sessions—dubbed "tutorials"—at Reagan's home, but they didn't work. Conrad was a crusty, professorial type who laid down his principles and never made them come to life.

They may have come from the same profession, but Reagan and Conrad didn't connect. Reagan couldn't grasp whatever Conrad was lecturing about. It was all so distant and rote. Reagan refused to go on with Conrad.

This was a daunting setback. Faced with what seemed like an impossible impasse, Salvatori began to think of replacing Reagan with former Governor Goodwin Knight. Nofziger was against the move. He was a Reagan man. But that didn't solve the problem, although Nofziger didn't think it was as dire as Salvatori did.

Then a possible solution presented itself.

9

The Call

Behavioral psychology is, to oversimplify the definition completely, the study of why people do one thing and not another, how they feel about it, and what you can learn from studying their actions. For instance, Stan's doctoral dissertation analyzed the mail—and there was a lot of it on both sides of the question—that came into the Senate regarding Senator Joe McCarthy, the extremely controversial 1950s Wisconsin anti-Communist. Stan analyzed the language used, the sentence structure, the level of rage, all of it, then decided which letter-writer posed a real threat, who was venting steam, or who was just harmlessly crazy, coming up with basic threat-evaluation language. Hint: If someone writes, "I know where you live," you need to start worrying.

Two unheralded behavioral psychologists, Stan and I were still in our thirties, and we had nothing in particular to recommend us for such important work except some willing traits and uncompromised discipline that wouldn't appear on any list of professional requirements for political consultants in the mid-1960s. That is to say, we belonged to an exotic field of soft science just beginning to have a social impact—frightening to some, exciting to others.

We entered the story because of one of those interesting and odd twists of fate that happen once in a blue moon. You bump into a guy at the exact moment when he's looking for someone with your precise set of skills. The planets align—and it's kismet.

To understand the process, though, you have to go back to that night in October when I went to hear Reagan at the Brentwood elementary school. I was so impressed that I wanted him to run for office right then, unaware that he was already running for governor. I told Stan about it the next day, and Stan, seeing my enthusiasm, said that he would pass it along.

I knew that he was connected to important Republican movers and shakers. It happened, at the time, that we were doing a job for the Republican State Central Committee, so we had access to the business end of the Republican Party. (The Republican State Central Committee, not an official arm of the party, was chartered to perform services for the party—vetting candidates, testing the impact of certain policies, etc.).

Along those lines, we were researching voter motivation: Why do people prefer Candidate A over Candidate B; what is it that makes one guy more appealing than another? Are there key words that resonate more deeply with some people or with particular blocs of voters?

The man who had hired us for the voter study was Dr. Robert Krueger, a light physicist (by which I mean that he studied the physics of light, not that he was dangerously underweight) who, like us, was a frustrated conservative Republican. He had worked to reelect Eisenhower in 1956, stayed active in politics, and felt disappointed and betrayed when Goldwater lost. All of the other big academics in his field—the left-leaning Democratic physicists—cold-shouldered him for his open partisanship. Apparently it was okay to promote a Democrat openly, but working on the other side of the street was verboten. It was practically the same story that we ran into in our academic careers. Never mind that Dr. Krueger had his own planning and research company and that he helped develop space capsules for

NASA. No, that wasn't good enough; he could help get us into space, but he couldn't keep his own academic reputation aloft. You had to agree politically—otherwise it didn't count.

By the late '50s, Krueger was fed up. The same embedded mindset drove him to seek his own solution—which is how he came to the RAND Corporation, NASA, and finally to his own company, Planning Research Corporation (PRC). He branched out and began working with local Republican committees, which inevitably put him in direct touch with important Republicans, including Henry Salvatori.

A tall, impressive man with dark hair graying at the temples, Krueger wound up doing a lot of important work for the government, and he satisfied his soul by helping local Republicans. Krueger was one of the "wise men" in Southern California's Republican Party; he was trusted and considered an opinion maker.

We had begun preparing various position papers for the Republican State Central Committee, so when Stan asked for some academic help in the business community, they suggested Dr. Krueger, who had started his own private think tank, PRC, which he had spun off from the RAND Corporation.

Although we didn't know it at first, Stan and I were following a well-trodden path when we broke with academia. We did some work for PRC, appraising potential candidates working in sensitive areas. It was a humbling experience, knowing that careers depended on our opinions.

In one instance, Krueger asked us to evaluate five men trying to get security clearance for important government work. They were going to be dealing with ciphers and top-secret material. He wanted us to determine which of them could pass a polygraph test—by nature, a humiliating experience.

We didn't know what they were going to be doing or any of the technical details related to their work, but we could discover how they made decisions and how they arrived at their conclusions. We could evaluate them as people, their executive skills, their ability to act under pressure. As it happened, we singled out two men whom we found flawed, unable to stick to one version of a story. And we were right. They didn't pass the polygraph.

After that, we were golden.

When it came to the Republican State Committee, Krueger wanted us to look into the question of voter motivation. Initially, he had been impressed by Stan's analysis of the 1965 Watts riots, which he had undertaken for the same committee. Dr. Krueger then asked Stan to write some position papers for possible Republican candidates and to write some articles for the state Republican newsletter.

Stan and I, as a team, were bound by more than political instincts and ideological preferences—we were professional partners, and even more than that we were friends. So after that October night in Brentwood, when I told Stan about Reagan and insisted that he tell someone immediately, he naturally passed along my enthusiasm to Krueger, his guru.

That conversation would bear fruit a few months later, when Henry Salvatori and Spencer-Roberts were in a panic over Reagan's perceived flaws as a candidate and went to Krueger to ask for his help. He immediately thought of us.

After that catastrophic initial press conference, Reagan began traveling up and down the state, using that same text, talking about government waste in Washington. Now, however, because of the enormity of that one gaffe, the press coverage had grown toxically condescending. He'd give his speech, then the reporters popped up with patronizing questions. The big favorite was always something along the lines of: Isn't it presumptuous to think that someone without a shred of experience in public life could be governor? To which he'd say, in his bumbling, folksy way: "Well, I was head of a labor union for many years"; or: "State government could use a fresh pair of eyes, someone who isn't jaded." His answers vanished into a fog of skepticism.

It wasn't a winning strategy. Nor was it curing the problem. George Christopher, of course, couldn't have been happier about the foundering Reagan. Spencer-Roberts was getting feedback from the field that the candidate was muffing too many questions, jumbling too many figures, confusing the office of governor with the office of president. He'd veto this and veto that—not quite understanding that as governor he would have to answer to the State Legislature. He couldn't rule by fiat.

In fact the only people rooting for Reagan at this stage were Pat Brown's people. Their polling was indicating that the governor would have a far tougher time with Christopher than against Reagan. Of course, at this stage we were rooting for Brown to win the Democratic primary against Yorty. We thought he'd be a much easier opponent for us. We turned out to be right; Brown's people (and their polling) turned out to be wrong.

That's when Bill Roberts and Henry Salvatori went to Bob Krueger and said that they needed someone to "educate" Reagan about California politics. Krueger said he just happened to know a couple of young psychologists who could probably get the job done.

The call came from campaign headquarters. It was a Monday morning in late January 1966. Stan and I were summoned to the Spencer-Roberts command center on Wilshire Boulevard in downtown Los Angeles. We knew that Spencer-Roberts was in the campaign management business, and they were pretty successful and pretty selective about picking the help.

However, we were not unprepared. We knew that the Reagan campaign had hit a wall. It had been almost three weeks since that fateful stumble on television. He was always popular with an audience—his great gift—but Reagan always managed to mangle a few details, and he invariably rambled on far too long about small issues.

Someone had to save this campaign for the Southern California wing of the party. That was the mission. That's what Bob Krueger told us when he delivered our marching orders, explaining the full nature of the crisis, making clear that we had to rescue Reagan from his own bad habits.

It was a tall order.

Waiting for us in the conference room of the downtown head-quarters was the tip of the Reagan spear: Bill Roberts, in his customary pose—sprawled out on a couch—a big, floppy man in a bespoke suit, who wore what we came to recognize as a habitual skeptical frown; and then there was his sleeker and leaner partner, Stu Spencer, perfectly at home in his ready-to-wear three-hundred-dollar suit—three hundred dollars being a lot to shell out for a suit in the 1960s. Also in the room was the chief Reagan advocate, the soft-spoken aristo-crat Holmes Tuttle, a man bathed in an aura of success like expensive cologne. The rough wildcatter Henry Salvatori was pacing like a lion, his clothes as fine as Tuttle's and Roberts, but his hands callused and stained, the mark of a man who had spent his life working on oil rigs.

"We want to help."

I could see them sizing us up. Well, that's why we were there. This whole enterprise was a Hail Mary, a desperate last-ditch effort to keep Spencer-Roberts from jumping off the Reagan ship. But they were running short of patience. There was lingering affection for George Christopher, maybe even some guilt for jilting him in favor of the movie star. Besides, they were probably thinking that Christopher wasn't completely a lost cause. They could always give him a quick spit shine and make him sparkle. It wouldn't have taken much to get Spencer and Roberts to switch sides. They admired Reagan, they even liked him, but the two young operators had taken a long leap of faith when they agreed to manage his campaign. Now they were listening to the groaning complaints from the road about his performance. They were understandably nervous.

How much longer before the press stopped giving Reagan a pass? How much longer until they dropped their benevolent tolerance and the foibles and amateur gaffes turned into sharp critiques? This was, after all, a real contest for an important public office.

Tuttle and Salvatori weren't about to give up so easily. Of course the wobbly start unsettled them, but these were bottom-line, bare-knuckle business guys. They had dealt with balky startups before. They handled problems, got under the hood, tinkered, made things work—that's how you succeeded in business.

"*Can* you help?"

They knew our background, if they didn't totally understand it, in teaching and researching. They just couldn't figure out what two behavioral psychologists could do to stanch the bleeding. If a former legislator couldn't help, what on earth could we do? But they also knew we were rare birds—academics who were also reliable conservative Republicans.

"We don't know," we answered (or, rather, Stan answered). "We'd have to see him in action. Get to know him a little."

There wasn't much time.

His next appearance was at a fund-raising dinner at the Beverly Hilton in Inglewood. A full house. Not surprising even then—Reagan could always fill the house. He had that winning, easy way. We stood in the back, listening. Not the way I listened in the Brentwood Elementary School, as a star-struck acolyte, but listening closely, critically, analytically, like professionals.

Reagan spoke about limited government (for it) and the abuses of federal bureaucracy (against them). He spoke against Lyndon Johnson's recently enacted Medicare program, saying that Americans would "awake to find we have socialism." He decried the "stultifying hand of government regulation and interference." The upshot, he predicted, would be, inevitably, totalitarianism.

He told familiar anecdotes, repeating the story told to him by a judge about a woman who came up before the judge seeking a divorce. She was young, with six children, and pregnant. Under the judge's questioning it became clear that the husband didn't share his wife's desire for a divorce. The husband earned $250 a month as a laborer, but by divorcing him the wife would get $80 more from the Aid to Dependent Children program. In other words, the government, in its blind, blundering way, was making it easier for families to break up, with all the damage that would cause to the children, than to stay together.

Such lessons were clear to Reagan: We were slipping into a nightmare world of unintended consequences. Our choices were clear, he insisted. We have to fight against this slippery slide into lazy forfeiture of our freedoms. "You and I have a rendezvous with destiny," he proclaimed. "We can preserve for our children this, the last best home of man on earth, or we can sentence them to take the first step into a thousand years of darkness. If we fail, at least let our children, and our children's children say of us that we justified our brief moment here. That we did all that could be done."

It was stirring. It was always stirring. But it featured zero material about California. It was a variation of the speech that he had delivered to the GE workers and to uncounted Chamber of Commerce dinners when he was on the rubber-chicken circuit. It was the speech that made my eyes well up in that little school room. But it wasn't going to get any votes in California. Californians had very specific concerns: agriculture, water, transportation, the economy, the state of the universities—in particular the state of their children, whom they had sent there to be educated and who were now tearing down everything in sight.

After the speech, Stan and I went out to dinner and talked through the question of Ronald Reagan, the perfect candidate with the imperfect approach. We agreed immediately that he needed to be re-educated, refocused, put on track. We knew exactly what we needed to do—but we didn't know yet if he would work with us. We also agreed that if we were to be able to have an effect on the candidate, we would have to isolate him from everyone else, all the so-called "experts," which we saw as chaotic influences pulling him in different directions. We had to have him alone.

We realized that it was highly unlikely that the professional handlers would agree to that. After all, proximity is the coin of the realm in any political activity. Let your guy out of your sight for five minutes, and someone else is likely to grab him, fill his head with God knows what, and give him back to you changed in some frightening way and looking at you as if you're some stranger he's never met before.

Stan and I decided there was only one way to go: as the Marines say, "Hey, diddle diddle! Straight up the middle." No flanking attacks, no polite throat-clearing, no hemming and hawing. Give it to Reagan's people straight. They'd either buy it, or they wouldn't. Either way, we'd know quickly, and we could get on with our lives.

So we went back to the "wise men" and described the dinner at Inglewood, Reagan's speech, and our reaction to it. We talked about the lack of focus, the need to impose discipline, the need to focus on the needs of California's voters. As they nodded in agreement, we sprung our five demands:

1. The campaign would stop for three days.
2. Stan and I would meet with Reagan for those three days.
3. We would meet in private. Isolation. Ronald Reagan, Stan Plog, and Ken Holden. No telephones. No interruptions. No tip-offs to the press about where we were or what we were up to.
4. If we got along and the results were satisfactory, Reagan would sign on with us. Period. We would not work for Spencer-Roberts, we would not report to the Kitchen Cabinet, we would not be handled by anyone.
5. None of this was negotiable. Take it, or leave it.

Salvatori, who wasn't used to being talked to like that, went through the roof. It couldn't be done, he said. He wasn't going to turn his candidate over to us for three days without adult supervision. There had to be someone there to oversee the sessions.

I repeated the part about these conditions being nonnegotiable.

Salvatori's face turned red. I was not some milquetoast academic. I had been in two wars, I had been through typhoons. Salvatori might have been a tough old oil-field knockabout, but the worst he could do here was yell at me; I wasn't going to cave, and I was not about to compromise. The issue arose of who was going to answer to whom. Did we report to Bill Roberts or Holmes Tuttle? Salvatori wanted us to report to Spencer-Roberts, and I saw that as a deal breaker.

Stan knew my temper and tried to cool me off, but Salvatori stood his ground, grabbing the edge of his desk with those rough, oil-rigger hands, the veins on his neck bulging.

"Who the hell do you think you are?" he shouted.

I was pretty cocky in those days, and I didn't see the point of caving—not when the whole state was at stake. Nor did I see a downside to losing the whole gig. "I'll tell you who I am," I said, "I'm one of two guys who can save this campaign, that's who I am."

Stan was trying to pull me away, saying softly that we could work it out, but I had my dander up, and I wasn't going to let us get bullied out of something this important. I was prepared to fight or quit the whole project. It was quite a showdown, but fortunately it was Henry Salvatori who backed down. He had seen the lukewarm attitude of Spencer-Roberts, and he could contrast that with our passionate commitment. I also think that in his heart he preferred dealing with people who stood up to him. He, Tuttle, and the Spencer-Roberts people recognized that we were immovable on the subject. It was a measure of the desperate state of the campaign that they agreed to our terms.

First, of course, we had to find out if we could work with Reagan—and if he could work with us. Until that was settled, there was no point even in talking about the next stage. So, before we did anything else we had to meet the candidate. It would be the crucial test of the chemistry. Roberts and Nofziger agreed to arrange a meeting at Reagan's Pacific Palisades home, the one described at the beginning of this book.

10

The Meeting

It was at that first person-to-person meeting with Ronald Reagan in late January at his Pacific Palisades home that we saw for ourselves just how alone he was.

There he was, standing in the doorway in his casual sports jacket, perfectly pressed slacks, and dazzlingly shy smile. He lit up the room, and we knew exactly why we were there.

"Can I get you fellas anything?" he said.

He was a gentleman always—an ideal American aristocrat. But an aristocrat whose nobility came not from inherited privilege but from a combination of Midwest breeding, family nurture (at least Nelle's), and an adult life spent in the spotlight.

After a moment of introductions and a polite exchange of pleasantries, we got down to business.

"We wanted to see how you work," I began. "Where do you get your ideas?"

He and Nancy exchanged that shy, knowing smile that comes to people who are deeply committed to each other.

He excused himself and left the room for a moment; when he came back, he was holding a big, overflowing shoebox containing newspaper clippings, magazine articles, his own notes. The box was packed with material, most of it about the ridiculous ways that big government was handling problems. You know: a report about a team of experts flown in from somewhere (at great expense) to study the mating habits of boll weevils, or a long study about the migrating patterns of ducks, or some other nonsense like that. It was the sort of stuff that William Proxmire, the long-serving Democratic senator from Wisconsin, later took great glee in lampooning with his celebrated Golden Fleece awards. Of course, it's also the kind of stuff that continues to flourish, regardless of who's in office or how mightily a senator, governor, or president might rail against it. Some things just don't change.

Reagan took pride in this collection that he had painstakingly clipped from the Defense Department, the Department of Agriculture, even the State Department. Everything in it, he said, showed the fallacy of bloated governance, the burden of ever-increasing taxes, and more and more regulation, more interference with business and schools and the effort of daily life. It was all there, in the shoebox. The method was touchingly amateurish, but it gleamed with a kind of dedicated sincerity.

"Well," I said, "you can't get all of your material from . . . that?"

Reagan looked a little confused, and turned to Bill Roberts, who didn't budge. Roberts remained sprawled on the couch, staying out of it all, with nothing to say, nothing to contribute.

Roberts perplexed us. He was supposed to be the campaign manager. He was the designated representative of the team that was supposed to manage the campaign of Ronald Reagan. From where we sat, we didn't see any management happening.

Reagan got some facts wrong. Okay, fine. Every candidate did that at some time. But where was the research team that would prepare him so he didn't make those kinds of mistakes? Reagan's speeches were repetitive and lacked focus. Okay, again, but where was his speechwriter? Did he even have a speechwriter? Reagan's appearances were uncoordinated and ill-chosen, with only a handful of people showing up. Okay, where were the travel guys and the booking agents and the advance team? Where, in other words, was his campaign management? Right at that moment, from where we sat, there was no campaign— just this disengaged guy sprawled out over the couch, watching us, listening to us, offering nothing.

Now that we were here in Reagan's home, Stan and I agreed that we liked him. We saw up close the remarkable qualities we had glimpsed from afar. But, natural as he was, he needed real, active guidance, not the unsympathetic apathy of Bill Roberts.

Nofziger, to his credit, was another story. He was a supporter—an authentic believer. But he didn't have any clout. And, at this meeting, faced with our specialized way of viewing the world, he didn't have any ideas—at least any informed ideas—to toss in the pot. He had a newspaper guy's flip sarcasm, and when he piped up it was to support an idea that someone else, either Stan or I, had proposed. Make no mistake: Nofziger was a nice man and a good guy, and he was more invested in what was going on than Spencer-Roberts. He was a Reagan man. But if Reagan fell by the wayside, he'd find himself another candidate.

Stan and I, though, were true believers. We were there for Reagan, and if we were the only ones who were, that was fine with us. We would go to the wall for him, if only we got the opportunity. If he went down in flames, well, Plog and Holden would go down in flames, too.

The next day we had it out again with Holmes Tuttle and Salvatori. Tuttle asked us what we thought, and we said that we could help.

"What kind of help?"

Our kind, we told him. The kind of help he needed—someone to steer him in the right direction when dealing with the press; someone to keep him focused when making a speech; and above all, someone to educate him about California politics—how it works, how much power a governor has, how different it is from national politics. He wanted to take on the country; our job was to prepare him for the smaller stage he would occupy before moving up to the main event.

"Well, go ahead."

Salvatori was fuming again. Once more he turned bright red as we reiterated our immovable conditions—three days alone, without telephones or interference; three full days of just us and the candidate. We'd have to bring him around again.

"Okay. You guys are the professionals," said Tuttle. "How do we do it?"

"We just do it," I said. I was the eager beaver, the hot pepper in this deal. "We have to stop the campaign, interrupt it for three days."

"Why three days?"

I had all the arguments ready. Salvatori's hostility at the initial meeting had prepared me, sharpened my thinking, focused my determination.

"One to get acquainted, two more to reorient the candidate. Any less and we couldn't get anything done. Any more and the press would be all over us. They'd sniff us out, tear into it and make a damning narrative or start dangerous rumors."

Three days was both the ideal and the limit.

It could work. We could easily explain it to the press: The candidate, we'd say, was taking a much-needed weekend. Everyone knew he had been sick, that he had a bladder infection. He had had it for weeks: a low-grade fever and a lot of trips to the bathroom. It didn't disable him, but it made everything that happened seem plausible.

There was one other condition. We insisted on a contract. Tuttle understood that. He was a businessman, and a contract made it an official business deal. We received $20,000 (1960s dollars no less), but we signed on for the whole ride. If this three-day tryout worked, it would be more than worth it.

We never saw Stu Spencer again in the primary. We dealt with Bill Roberts, but it was obvious he didn't like the whole deal—and he didn't like us. We understood that. Nobody likes having the power of absolute control pulled out from under him. He couldn't control us, so he disliked us and what we did. Years later, Spencer told Lou Cannon that neither he nor Roberts (nor Reagan, for that matter) understood what we were about. "They were honest guys, they were intellectual guys, they were maybe on the cutting edge of some kind of research," he said, "but the users didn't know how to use it, so there was no reason to screw around with it." This from a guy whose heart wasn't in the campaign from the beginning, who we never saw—and who never saw us in action—and who owes us more than he'll ever acknowledge.

But as a practical matter, it didn't matter what Spencer or Roberts thought about us. They were important, but Tuttle and Salvatori were the money guys, and in the end they called the shots. So they went to work again, scrubbing the schedule, arranging a place where we wouldn't be found, and informing Ronald Reagan that we were officially on the team.

PART TWO

11

Day One

Saturday, February 5, 1966

Among the other houses in Malibu, this one stood out. It was a millionaire's beach cottage, Cape Cod–style, something that seemed to come from the Twenties or Thirties, but, although seemingly modest at first glance, something so well-kept that it was head and shoulders above the crowd. I don't think I ever knew whose house it was—maybe it was Tuttle's summer place. What I do know is that Reagan's men seemed to be able to conjure up anything we wanted.

I picked up Stan at his place, and we drove down to the house together, going over the battle plan on the way. We had a concern, and it was one we had to get to right at the get-go: just how serious a man was Ronald Reagan? Was he really what he seemed to be, or was it an act? Would he stick to his guns when the going got rough, or was he merely playing at being a serious conservative? For instance, did Reagan really understand—as he said he did—the free-market philosophy of Friedrich Hayek, the twentieth-century Austrian economist who advocated a completely unfettered free market, or was he at heart just a movie-star dilettante? That was crucial to know—it was, in fact, the major question.

If Reagan failed this test, there was a good chance we wouldn't be interested in working with him. We weren't the only ones on trial that day.

We pulled up to the house in my old Chrysler and crossed into a different world. You could stare at the beachfront view, then turn 180 degrees and see acres and acres of green, manicured land, all stretching off into a beautiful morning—and it was beautiful. It was the California that lured ambitious Midwesterners like the three of us who were about to sit down and try to change history.

Reagan was waiting for us in his always elegant casual style—sports jacket, cream-colored shirt, slacks. The usual formal distance that Reagan maintained between himself and the rest of the world—the emotional moat he tended to live behind—had shrunk. He wasn't wearing a tie.

He further loosened the mood: "Call me Ron."

"Stan."

"Ken."

Stan and I shucked our own neckties, drank the coffee he had waiting, then sat down in the living room and tried to ignore the view of the Pacific Ocean just outside the bay window.

I couldn't help thinking that this was a different Pacific than the one I feared would swallow me up in 1945. This Pacific backdrop held a different kind of promise.

Reagan leaned back in a chaise longue. Stan and I asked one or two questions—polite icebreakers, like "How's Nancy?"—but then the candidate held up a hand, stopped us in our tracks, turned the tables:

"Tell me a little about yourselves," he said.

He wanted to know who he was dealing with. Obviously, he didn't trust the Spencer-Roberts briefing, nor should he have really, based on what we could already decipher from the prior encounter. But now we were here, and he wanted to know, on the deepest personal level, the level where he operated best, just what kind of men we were. If he could know us, he could trust us. If he could trust us, he could work with us. If he could work with us, some good might come from all this.

Reagan, of course, was easy to talk to. We could tell he liked hearing life stories like mine and Stan's. He was always trying to connect to you with stories. That was how he understood the world.

I went first, and told him the same story I've already told in these pages. About my family name. About my doughty ancestor Randall Holden and how he helped found the colony of Rhode Island and signed the Portsmouth Contract in the seventeenth century. I told him how I grew up listening at the air vent upstairs to my grandfather talking about the massacre of George Armstrong Custer and his men at the Little Big Horn, the great trauma of his generation.

Then I told him this story: Every year my parents drove to Pennsylvania to visit my grandfather at his retirement farm. In those days, cars didn't have seat belts. Once, as we were driving there on a gravel road at about fifty miles an hour, the back door blew open, and I flew out onto the road. I was about three at the time. When my parents scooped me up and took me to my grandfather's house, he stood me on the kitchen table and picked gravel out of my hands and face like it was buckshot. I was shaken but relatively unhurt, and my grandfather admired the way I dealt with the whole thing

"I always knew he was hardheaded," he said, laughing.

It was the sort of insight that Reagan needed. Kids had it tough, and so they had to be tough. I knew that he processed it that way. He was always connecting the dots.

I told him about St. Joe and working a paper route. I told him how I grew up around guns, which we considered to be no more than tools. The guns in my parents' house were always kept loaded, so you learned not to pick one up without checking the chamber. It was a potentially deadly business, so there couldn't be any doubt. I eventually taught my own kids the same weapon discipline.

I told him I had been a ham radio operator, I told him about joining the Merchant Marine at seventeen. I told him about the *Nancy Hanks*. I told him about my war.

I told him about going to school on the GI Bill, about enlisting for the Korean War because I thought it was the right thing to do, about how I took courses for an advanced degree in psychology while still in the Air Force. I told him about UCLA, about the atmosphere there, about how Stan and I had met, and, like orphans in the liberal storm, how we had stayed true to our principles, which were his principles, too.

It lasted quite a while, maybe an hour, maybe more. Reagan was a good listener, and I told him things about myself that Stan had never even heard. By the time I finished, we had moved out to the lawn chairs on the beach. The weather, even in February, was balmy.

Reagan had absorbed my story and found not merely the common threads between us—Midwestern self-sufficiency, solid work ethic, a climb to make something of yourself, a call for a greater sacrifice—he also got some insight into a world just over his own horizon. He recognized himself in these details.

It was time for lunch. The three of us drove up to a local deli and bought some food, then took a walk in the sand. As we strolled along the sand, I felt there was something deeply satisfying about this particular technique of familiarization. There were no telephone interruptions and no campaign aides breaking in with whatever they thought urgent—just the three of us and the sound of the waves breaking on the sand, an occasional gull shrieking. Malibu worked its magic on us. As we sat there, letting the effects of the sea and the stories sink in, Ron—as he preferred to be called—gazed off into the far horizon and said with a sigh, "Fellas, this is the life!"

Stan's story had the extra kick of an angle that was sure to appeal to Ron, a gritty kind of glamour. And just like my story had revealed aspects of me that Stan hadn't known, so did his reveal things he'd never told in the years we'd been friends. He spilled his guts for Reagan, though.

For the first time, I realized how poor Stan had been as a kid and how that poverty had galvanized him, how determined he was to work his way out of that ditch. He told us about the father who'd disappeared, the stepfather who'd given him his surname and the great advice about combining academic excellence with mastery of the trombone. He told us how he'd played his 'bone in three Elvis Presley movies and two Lewis and Martin pictures, not to mention Bing Crosby's *White Christmas*.

Those credits got Reagan's attention. "Really?" he said. "No kidding?"

Ron was impressed.

"Yeah, I landed a nice gig doing sideline work as a band member in a bunch of pictures," said Stan.

Ron was enchanted. Expecting a couple of dry, data-driven academics, he had, instead, stumbled on someone who spoke his language, understood his show-business world—and understood politics as well.

To be totally honest, though, Stan had to break the bubble. He told Ron that he was really unhappy as a Hollywood musician. He hated the recording sessions and the TV work, so he joined the Air Force and spent his tour of duty playing in the Air Force band. When he was discharged he went back to school—and not just any school: Harvard. He earned scholarships and got his PhD in psychology.

When Stan finished—I don't think he took as long as I did—Ron beamed at us. "Quite a story," he said. "Quite a pair of stories. I was expecting a couple of eggheads. But you boys have been out in the world. The real world. You come completely unexpected."

We *had* been out in the real world. We hadn't been stuck in the ivory tower gazing at our navels. We were pleased that Reagan had seen that, that he *got* who we were and what we were about. But that, satisfying as it was, wasn't what put a light in our eyes. It was what came afterward. Ron was relaxed enough to tell us his own story, how he had been ostracized, how he had run out of possibilities on the silver screen and then taken his leap into politics. We were champion storytellers, but no one told a story like Ron.

"The first day I was in Hollywood—right after I signed my first movie contract after the radio days—I heard a knock on the front door of my apartment. Well, I opened it and there was this young man holding a bloody dog in his arms. The young man had found the dog in the street, apparently hit by a car, and he was going door-to-door trying to find the owner. I think he eventually did find the owner in another apartment, and the dog did recover. But I realized right afterward—and this is after the door is closed and I am suddenly struck by what happened, like a double-take in a movie—that young man was a movie star. That was my introduction to Mickey Rooney. He lived right across the street. And there he was, a young man holding a wounded dog in his arms. In Hollywood, when you answer a knock on your door, you just never know who's going to be on the other side."

He still had that wide-eyed innocent awe at the wonder of his world: You open your door, and there's a movie star outside!

The three of us understood as we sat in the afternoon light of that first long day that Reagan had been persuaded into this race but that some of the people who had initially backed him, were turning on him. Holmes Tuttle was still there on his old friend's side, and he could carry a lot of people with him. But the mercenaries Spencer and Roberts had all but given up. They saw Reagan's race for the governorship as a short-term gig. They were in the game for the long haul, and they couldn't let an imperfect candidate drag them down.

"They don't trust me," Reagan said.

We went back inside. As we sat in that plush living room, it went unsaid, but we knew that we were all outcasts. That's what gave us such a comfort zone on that beach in Malibu. We were all three outsiders, staring through the same bay window.

"We have work to do," I said.

We started to feel at home in that little Cape Cod house by the sea. Already, on that first afternoon, we had established a routine. We knew where to find the coffee and where the bathrooms were and—a subtle but important point—how long to work before taking a break. The sheer casual intimacy of it all came with truly rare speed.

Ron also still had that bladder infection that dogged him throughout the rest of the campaign, so we tried to anticipate when to call for a bathroom break. It dawned on me that, in a very short span of time, we had developed the unspoken sensitivity of foxhole buddies. This one likes his tea plain, that one has a sweet tooth, Ron has to have his breaks.

All it took was the shedding of defenses. Embracing a certain degree of candor, along with a preexisting fusion of beliefs. That was enough. We bonded.

The picnic table in the back served as the perfect spot for lunch, and the weather was fair-sailing—a spring-like day in mid-winter with the temperature in the sixties. Even the people who passed us on the beach seemed to sense our need for complete and splendid isolation. They just walked on by.

But now it was time for work.

Our first order of business was to test Ron's beliefs. Could he be talked out of his declared conservatism? That always posed a big problem with politicians. They usually recognized that taking a strong position automatically alienated a given segment of the electorate. So, instead of sticking to their guns, they slid into a fuzzier stance on an issue before them, chewing away at the core belief until, finally, there was no real belief—just another politician trimming his sails depending on which way the wind was blowing.

But not Ron.

He believed that a man can be against big government and still support a compassionate society. You had to encourage charity, fight waste, demand accountability. The sloppy ways of government waste offended him deeply. Bureaucrats playing with other people's money! He stood for cutting government, plain and simple; that alone would eliminate the worst abuses.

This wasn't just a trope that he adopted for popular consumption. He had read enough and studied enough to be sure of his ground. He cited the individual freedom demanded by social philosophers like Thomas Paine. He had read *The Rights of Man* and *Common Sense* and opposed the philanthropic tyranny that, he believed, came as the inevitable byproduct of big government.

As far as his economic theories went, he traced his intellectual lineage all the way back to the Enlightenment, when writers like Locke, Voltaire, and Montesquieu first linked political and economic freedom. He quoted them and he quoted Frédéric Bastiat.

Never heard of him? Neither had we. Stan and I had done our reading, but Bastiat was new to us. The obscure nineteenth-century Frenchman tickled Ron, who explained that a wicked sense of humor came with Bastiat's free-market beliefs. In his *Economic Sophisms*, Bastiat posed a satirical parable that became famous as the candle makers' petition, in which the candle makers' guild urged the French government to block out the light of the sun to prevent unfair competition with their product.

The object of the story, one that Reagan heartily agreed with: It was ridiculous for government to try to control everything, and industry had to accept its limitations, instead of looking for help from Big

Brother. Another absurdist Bastiat joke: He advocated cutting off everyone's right hand. That way, work would be more difficult, thus more valuable, thereby increasing overall wealth. You don't have to be a deep thinker to see how Bastiat's barbs at government regulation would find a receptive audience in Ronald Reagan.

This guy had not only done his homework, he had done postgraduate work on the obscure as well as known philosophers in this field. Nancy said that he was a great reader, but we didn't appreciate how deeply he'd gone. He dug out these thinkers like he dug out his shoebox of clippings. As we probed, we got to see the man's method and his quirks. He always appreciated a sensible and pragmatic—and humorous—approach to a problem. He liked to take a complicated puzzle and reduce it to a simple, clear axiom that the average person could understand.

For instance: If you spend more than you make, you will fall into debt. If you can live without something you can't afford, virtue demands that you pass it by. Many of these rules came from his own life experience. He had trouble with the IRS when he was paying a 90 percent marginal tax rate, so he examined government policies with a jaundiced eye.

Of course he didn't agree with John Maynard Keynes, the British economist who advocated that government should stimulate a flagging economy by spending on credit. No, his was a Midwestern version of frugal economics. He saw the beauty of New Englanders' habit of "talking cheap," always downgrading their possessions to ward off jealousy and prevent hubris. It was the hard remnant of the old Calvinist work ethic that lingered in America's heartland like a first love.

Adam Smith, he believed, had come closest to the truth: Rational self-interest in a free-market economy leads to economic well-being. From Locke, Reagan derived his clear connection to religion. Locke had argued that the existence of God is as knowable as mathematics and with the same precision; we just can't see it because human understanding is limited. It was a little breathtaking.

The media had dismissed Reagan as a dilettante, an amateur on the political stage. But he was far deeper and far more learned than any of his critics.

At the end of the day, Stan and I concluded that his beliefs stood on the solid rock of conviction and extensive self-education. He had not come to his opinions by whim or inclination or through some easily administered indoctrination. He had arrived at this place by devoted study and rigorous thought.

But how did all of this economic and philosophical and theological passion translate into such high ideological certainty? How did the daily business of American politics present itself to the highly opinionated and informed candidate who sat so serenely before us?

It was self-evident—right there, reported in the newspapers, broadcast on the news. He had collected the evidence like autumn leaves, folding them neatly into his magic shoebox.

12

Day Two

Sunday, February 6, 1966

It was a half-hour trip to Malibu, and we plotted the day like associate professors working out a syllabus. I had had breakfast at home—I needed the time alone to think, to evaluate what I'd heard, to plan for the next session. Stan picked me up, and then we drove down to the beach discussing the day's schedule.

We agreed that the main job was to organize the candidate's chaotic speeches and thoughts so that he presented a coherent case for himself. Reagan was too eager to overplay his hand and deliver everything he knew in one great gust of wind. We had to get him to minimize that tendency.

The shoebox bulged with his clippings: a noticeable cost overrun on a simple contract to supply trucks to the army; a large cost overrun on a contract to rehabilitate a historic monument; an even larger overrun on the development of a new jet fighter for the Air Force. Each clipping carried an implicit outcry against unfathomably sloppy government management.

There were also stories about petty squabbles within the government—over, for instance, coming up with a more genteel name for a toilet—and all the stalling tactics employed to slow down services and jack up costs. All the while, essential projects could never seem to get done cleanly.

From the perspective of that shoebox—albeit a shoebox filtered through the eyes of an aroused conservative—it was easy to depict government as petty, dysfunctional, and in pretty bad need of a large overhaul.

Reagan had one simple conviction: If we stuck to the unadorned language of the Constitution, America could right itself. He wanted to eliminate bureaucratic interference with basic freedom and force a sleek new way of doing things. It was a matter of applying sensible ideological techniques. The secret was a kind of mental trick. Reagan had tidy psychological habits: He could arrange items in neat categories and solve problems without allowing himself to get bogged down in complicated details. He saw the world as perfectly accessible to his own understanding and to a rational spirit.

We understood where these beliefs and convictions were coming from. Not just out of a shoebox, but from real economic thinkers and philosophers, from Locke to Bastiat to Hayek. But there was the problem of delivery. A candidate for governor couldn't unleash a flash flood of arcane economic theory on an unsuspecting audience. Reagan wasn't always showing it, but he was awash in his own erudition. He had to be toned down. We needed to devise a method for him to present his case in a simple, disciplined way—a way that would allow him to avoid coming out looking either foolish or pedantic.

There was also his confusion of federal and state politics. His eye might be on the larger prize, but we had to pivot his mindset away from national politics. He wasn't running for president of the nation (yet). He was running for governor of California, and he had to start acting like it.

Part of the problem was that Reagan had been working without a staff, without researchers who could organize issues, plot positions, pinpoint important details, give him solid facts. In other words, everything that he needed to be a plausible candidate. We, on the other hand, had in our headquarters in Van Nuys the kind of people who could do the research, isolate the issues, condense the findings into digestible lumps, and feed them to the candidate in a way that he could absorb quickly, then toss them out in the blink of an eye to whatever audience he was addressing.

Lunch at the picnic table, a delightful cool afternoon with the usual passersby looking, recognizing Reagan, but also recognizing that this was a moment out of the limelight, and so they respected his privacy.

We were a very cozy group, cleaning up the papers and plates with meticulous care, aware that we were custodians of someone else's property.

Reagan was clearly enjoying himself. "This is why we love California," he said, gazing off in the distance, past the ocean, as if seeing something no one else could see.

We saw something that everyone else could see but couldn't name. Reagan was a very graceful man. Where he stood and how he got there always seemed to be perfectly natural. Just the business of sitting down at the lunch table looked eloquent. He fit into the chair perfectly, leaving no uncomfortable gaps—a creature who carried himself as nature intended. That was how he fit into the world, that was how the world saw him. But then he was a natural athlete as well as an actor.

But time was short—three days minus one and a half.

Back to work.

In his orderly world, Ron had devised a technique for keeping his thoughts and positions on issues in discrete form: He put them on index cards. He wrote down notes with a felt-tipped pen, and then he shuffled them around when he had to write a speech. He stuffed the index cards into the inside pocket of his suit jacket, and, unlike modern politicians reading from a teleprompter, he'd pull out his five-by-eight cards and riffle through them until he found his place on any given subject. Needless to say, it was not a very effective way to deliver a speech. It broke the rhythm, and it made him look unprepared. When he couldn't find the right card right away, it made him look vaguely befuddled, the "amiable dunce" of Clark Clifford's mean-spirited (and wildly off-target) later characterization.

But Ron liked the card's tactile feel—something substantial written down on something solid—like the feel of a script, which he knew how to handle. For example, education. Do we really need Washington bureaucrats deciding what our schools should teach? Isn't it better to decide such matters closer to home?

It was a system Stan and I could work with, with some modifications. Since Stan and I agreed to take on the Reagan contract (less than a month earlier, remember), our BASICO staff, all of them smart and hard-working men and women, many of them working on advanced degrees in a wide variety of subjects, had been hard at work winnowing through the myriad concerns of California's voters. They had pored through every copy of every newspaper in the state, from the *L.A. Times* and the *Sacramento Bee* and the *San Francisco Chronicle* right down to the local community papers in towns of a few hundred people. They had combed through the articles, and the reports of community meetings; they had scanned the letters to the editor, gradually building up a base of data. What were the people of California concerned about? What were they talking about? What were they writing to their local paper about?

They added and aggregated, piled statistic on statistic. Then, like cowboys in the Old West isolating the calves they needed in the vast herd, they began cutting out the issues that they identified as the ones that Reagan needed to be expert on. They lassoed them, dragged them to the side, and slapped a brand on them. If, indeed, we were back in the Old West, the brand would have been a simple one to remember: "RR!" it would have read.

At the time, I told Reagan: "You won't have to worry. We have people who will gladly do the work and put accurate material in your hands." No more shoeboxes—it was time for shoe leather.

In the end, our research concluded that there were seventeen or eighteen issues that lay at the core of the race for governor. Some were intensely local, to be mentioned only when the candidate visited a specific part of the state; some were of interest only in Northern California and not in Southern California, or vice versa; and some were on the minds of every voter no matter where he or she lived. As Reagan campaigned across the state, we listened carefully to the questions asked and tweaked our research.

Every fact relating to every issue was checked, double-checked, triple-checked. There would be no more inadvertent gaffes like the misstatement about the 15.1 percent welfare rate. If he said that California employed 10.4 teachers for every 150 kids—not that I can remember the real figures—that number would have to be right, down to the decimal. Reagan simply couldn't afford to be wrong again. And we certainly didn't want him to be wrong because of some minuscule bit of data that we might have mistyped.

Once we had the issues isolated and fact-checked, we arranged the work into cards that fit into loose-leaf binders. Eventually we produced three volumes: one book of facts, one book of conservative positions (something like philosophical rocks), and another book of policy ideas, which he would promote for the future.

Everything was on five-by-eight-inch individual cards loaded into the books. The cards had holes punched into the sides so that Reagan could take the cards out of the notebooks when he needed to address a particular subject: economics, education, public safety, social standards, values.

We also produced a series of discussion cards that covered the pros and cons of each issue. In other words: Reagan's position on a particular subject, plus his opponent's position. Reagan didn't get that right away. If we said white, and our opponent said black, Reagan needed to be intimately familiar with the arguments for black as well as gray.

"Why study the contrary position?" he asked. "Why learn the other guy's arguments?"

"To counter them," I replied.

Not only did he have to be familiar with his opponent's argument, he had to know it inside out, better, if possible, than his opponent knew it. And he would know any other positions that might be floating around on a particular subject. That way we could see the flaws of history or reasoning, and he could smilingly eviscerate the other guy. Nothing could come as a surprise. Nothing could seem to make him uncomfortable. He would be prepared. He would be confident. And a prepared, confident candidate would be unflappable, serene in the knowledge that he could take whatever was thrown at him.

Reagan continued to resist a little.

"Do I really need to read all the ones that I don't accept, that are not my position?" he asked me again. It was almost as if the mere reading of left-wing ideas would somehow contaminate him.

Finally, of course, he got it. And he would use this knowledge to devastating effect in the primary campaign he was jumping into, as well as the race against Pat Brown.

That brought us to the third and final binder. We called it *The Creative Society,* and it laid out all of the ideas, plans, and programs that Reagan harbored for the future. For instance, he wanted to shift a lot of the responsibility for public assistance to private charities. In every case, he believed that it was better to enact a specific local remedy rather than leave the problem to a Washington bureaucrat to bungle the job.

In the end, he saw what we were getting at. He still wrote his own speeches, but now he would have the material at his fingertips. And because he was largely self-educated, a natural autodidact who absorbed information like a sponge, it would be easy for him to learn the contents of those index cards. It would give him the organizational and emotional lift he needed.

"Boys," he said, at the end of day two, smiling at us like an old friend, "I like the way this sounds."

On February 6, we took a slight break to observe Reagan's fifty-fifth birthday. We had a modest celebration at his house in Pacific Palisades. He didn't drink much, but this was an important occasion. He went behind the bar to make us a drink.

"What'll you have?" he asked.

I had a beer.

Stan asked for something exotic; I think it was called a Hawaiian Delight. Whatever it was, it called for gin, pineapple juice, and lime, and something else, and something else, and it involved measuring and mixing, getting the proportions just right, shaking, and probably a tiny paper umbrella.

A pained, mildly persecuted look came over Ron's face.

"Why don't you just have a beer," he said.

Stan had a beer and learned his lesson: He ordered umbrella drinks again in his life—but only when the bartender was actually a bartender.

13

Day Three

Monday, February 7, 1966

Ron would occupy the governor's mansion, of that we were certain, but he had to understand the nature of that job. He would be working in Sacramento, California, not Washington, D.C. He wouldn't have executive authority over the nation. He would govern one single state—a big prosperous, populous state—but just one state.

As chief executive of California, he couldn't slash budgets or dictate laws. Ultimately, he would have to answer to the State Legislature. Control was tightly limited. There were mandated costs built into that budget. Only a limited amount of discretionary spending would be available to him. The governor had great influence, he could sway public opinion, and he definitely could set a tone, but he had no overwhelming, decisive power. He couldn't just pick up the phone and bark orders that would immediately be carried out. The governor was more than a figurehead, certainly, but less than a chief.

So on the third day of our Malibu seminar, we moved Ronald Reagan's mind out of the White House—there would be time enough for that—and put him into the State House. Thus the education of Ronald Reagan marched into the senior hours of the California tutorial.

And we honed his performance as a candidate.

How to be a candidate? It's exhausting, and it's not as easy as it looks.

First, it's crucial to have your facts straight—keep them straight, no matter how long the day has been, or how exhausted you are, or how awful you feel because you have the flu and your brain feels like it's had its very last thought and would really rather go to sleep. We had all seen the danger of that particular pitfall. It's essential to have consistent policies and to maintain a coherent strategy. It helps to wear a pressed suit—preferably dark blue—and present a sober, smiling countenance. There are other factors, such as a native and unbroken spirit of optimism, but that quality our candidate had in his very DNA. It was, in fact, his singular shining gift. Call it the right temperament for office. He owned it.

Nevertheless, politics is a dangerous and tricky business. You can have all the gifts—look great, handle yourself with savoir faire, and be competent in public—but in the end it's a blood sport. Those other guys are out to skin you alive. Never mind that the other guy is a fellow Republican who will one day look you in the eye, grasp you by the hand, and declare himself your dearest friend and greatest ally; the fight is now, and the knives are there, if not always out in the open.

So we told him about staying cool.

You cannot, we told him, ever get angry. You don't want the voting public to see a man with a red face, sputtering and slamming the podium in rage. It'll look like you've lost control, which is a fatal impression. Above all, you don't want a reputation as a hothead. Many of the great undecided already suspect you're dangerously right-wing, a Goldwater with a Hollywood tan. If they see you explode, it'll confirm their worst suspicions and frighten them away. Voters are easily spooked, like the longhorns in old Westerns. It doesn't take much to make them stampede—away from you and toward the other guy.

Of course, there's an exception to every rule in politics, and there are moments too when a little show of temper—righteous temper—can do you a lot of good. And we told him about that, too.

Day three wound down and our tutorial came close to its end. Stan and I tried to present the choices to Reagan as a game of chess, admittedly a dry, bloodless metaphor for what we would soon come to see in the flesh. You make a move. The other guy makes a move. You see what he's up to—he's trying to kill your queen. It hurts. It makes you angry. But it's only a chess move. It's meant to catch you wrong-footed, to force you into making the fatal countermove. It's intended to attack your brain, make you crazy, make you try to get even instead of strategize. Between you and me, it's no chess game; it's a knife fight.

Reagan nodded, but he didn't get it—not completely, not then.

Stan was patient: "Look, Ron, this is a long chess game, this campaign. You have to understand that. The thing to do is to keep your head and make a smarter countermove. Shift the balance. Make the other guy make a mistake, make the fatal countermove."

Finally, he seemed to grasp what we were getting at. If they implied that you are stupid or even used that euphemistic insult, "uninformed," they were merely using chessboard tactics designed to throw you off your game.

I emphasized control. He had to remain in control at all times. He had to appear unruffled. He had to look unwounded, intact. Otherwise it gave credence to the attack.

But he was, after all, a professional actor, and people were always trying to belittle him for that, accusing him of being a dilettante, a mere performer acting like a politician, a stand-in for big money interests. Any way to break his concentration was fair game.

He did have amazing control, of course. And he had a real flair. He could turn the question inside-out, upside-down, so that the toxic end worked for him rather than against. Before he even declared his candidacy, on August 3, 1965, reporters snidely asked: "What would it be like for an actor to become governor of California?"

His good-natured answer was: "I don't know—I've never played governor before."

Naturally, the reporters laughed. Who wouldn't laugh? They were in on the joke. All of the poison instantly drained from the question. That's how to handle it, I told him. When you can, lighten it up, laugh at yourself. No one did it better. The quickest learner I have ever seen sat on the beach chairs in Malibu soaking up everything that we knew. He got it.

Later, at Occidental College, when students were howling against him, holding up signs: "Down with Reagan," "Down with Nancy," "Who wants Boraxo in Sacramento?" (Boraxo being the sponsor of *Death Valley Days*), Reagan ambled past the demonstrators with his jaunty gait and winning smile, waving brightly. When the crowd finally quieted down—and I'm quoting Dallek's book now—"Reagan turned to them and, referring to the Boraxo sign, said, "That may be only soap to you, but it's bread and butter to me." It lightened the moment and allowed him to proceed relatively uninterrupted.

Lunch on the beach on that last afternoon consisted of hamburgers, fries, and Cokes from a diner. We spoke like members of a commando team sending one of our number out on a mission. We briefed him, and briefed him again, particularly about the press. All you have to remember, we told him, is that every single one of them, whether they work for the smallest small-town rag or the *New York Times*, has only one goal in life—to advance their own careers by derailing yours. They're out to catch you in a mistake, trap you, set the ground for a blunder. If you look ridiculous, they look brilliant.

Every single one.

They'll never be on your side, but if you know how to deal with them, you can use them for your own ends.

Reagan could handle the press, but he needed to change his act. I've already mentioned that Stan and I noticed that he tended to ramble, to over-answer questions. It was a misguided attempt to counter the charge that he was an intellectual lightweight.

It wasn't the way to go. Make it brief, we told him. You don't have to address every little nuance of every question on every issue. You have to know when to give a nice, tight little clip so that it will shine on the six o'clock news. Don't go on too long. Whatever you do, don't bore people.

That's George Christopher's job, we told him. That drew a smile.

And we told him something else: You don't actually have to answer the reporters' questions. The First Amendment gives them the right to ask you the questions, but it doesn't mandate that you have to answer the question you were asked. Instead, you can give a friendly smile in the face of even the most unfriendly question, then turn it around, taking the poison out of it. Start with something like, "As I understand the question . . ." then give whatever answer you wanted to give in the first place. Look at it as a game. The great players enjoy it; they don't let the press or their opponents dominate the conversation.

Reagan was, of course, a great stealer of scenes. I saw this clearly when he and the other candidates all gathered for a picture. When the photographer was ready, Reagan held up his hand as if adjusting his necktie or moving someone closer. It gave him the appearance of being in control.

A serious candidate for high public office must possess a special kind of moxie.

Perhaps the most essential quality necessary to govern is something that can't be taught: the ability to judge people. Knowing whom to trust usually comes through painful spasms of trial and error. Not everyone who gives you his word is dependable. Not everyone who works on your campaign is wholeheartedly on your side.

There was his brother, Neil, "Moon," the West Coast vice president of the McCann-Erickson advertising agency. Moon had a lifetime rivalry with his brother, which he was on the edge of losing spectacularly, but Reagan still gave him a piece of the campaign's account. It soon became clear that Neil wasn't wholeheartedly on his side; at least he wasn't very effective. At one photo shoot, Neil insisted on retake after retake of a perfectly good campaign commercial. I had to intervene—seeing that the retakes were sapping Reagan's energy. Neil tried to shift the campaign's theme to something so low-key and off-pitch that his brother's voice seemed to vanish—no longer so firm on clamping down on college demonstrations, not quite so aggressive on tax reform, not so dedicated to countering government expansion.

In a way, Reagan was very naive. He retained that typical Midwestern value of trust. A handshake to him was a binding contract. He held onto an undying belief in the fundamental goodness of the average citizen. He believed that everyone should not only have a high code of honor but live by it.

However, he told us stories about Hollywood executives who promised large parts, a big career, then gave his career away, denigrated his gifts. He was supposed to get the lead in *Casablanca*, the role that made Humphrey Bogart a star in 1942. He was supposed to get the lead in *Twelve O'Clock High*, the role that launched Gregory Peck's career. Jack Warner loved him, loved him, loved him—but only saw him as an afterthought. It took him a long time to recognize the patterns. Reagan's mistake was being gullible and getting emotionally involved with unreliable people.

He learned that Hollywood worked by a kind of consensual mutual insincerity: air kisses, false enthusiasm, everyday backstabbing. There was nothing you could do about it. He wasn't mistreated per se. He still had some clout as a former leader of the Screen Actors Guild. The great Lew Wasserman, head of MCA, still took his calls, as did Jack

Reagan preparing for a TV spot. During one such session—perhaps this one—Reagan's brother, Neil, kept asking for a new and better shot. When he (Neil) turned and asked, "How is that?" I said, "That's fine," and the cameraman quickly shut everything down. Neil charged across the room and said, "Who are you?" I turned and walked away, leaving Neil repeating "Who was that? Who was that?" He was driving everyone—Reagan, the cameraman, and me—crazy with redundant good shots.

Warner, as did all the execs. They really liked him—or so they said. But he couldn't cash in all that affection for a fat screen role.

He had also been disappointed when he was fired by GE. Its president, Ralph J. Cordiner, had been Reagan's friend, had encouraged his free-wheeling speeches—until there was blowback from clients. Then Reagan was fired.

Reagan was about to learn that the air kisses and insincerity also played a role in politics. In a funny way, it made him shy, his gregarious Midwestern innocence worn down by disappointment. He was still able to appear in public, put on a show, handle a crowd, run for governor. But he didn't have many true friends. He was never not cautious.

And so, as President Reagan would say later, on a far bigger stage, with a great deal more at stake: Trust but verify.

PART THREE

14

The Fourth Day

We were all tired. Reagan still had that low-grade fever, but we came away from Malibu exhilarated—even with a sense of bright optimism.

The Malibu sessions turned out just the way we planned them. We were right to insist that we should have Reagan alone, without distractions, without interference, without the shadow of political nitpickers, hangers-on, and hawkers who buzzed like flies around a campaign. We got to see him plain. His grasp of our methods and our insights, to say nothing of the depth and breadth of his political convictions, impressed us.

We had spent a long weekend at the beach with the next governor of California. We were ready to plunge into whatever rough waters lay ahead.

As soon as we could arrange it, Stan and I met with Tuttle and Salvatori. They had agreed to our terms and signed our contract giving us access for the full primary campaign. We told them how good we felt about the Malibu sessions and that, if kept to a strict diet of campaign discipline, Ronald Reagan would surely succeed.

There was one caveat: He shouldn't be strangled. That is, the man should be allowed to breathe; he had great wit and intellect, and with the right help, with the full aid of our staff feeding him the raw meat

Reagan in the shadows beneath a poster that reads SEE THINGS CLEARLY—THE GOP.

that he needed, he would be fine on the stump. He was capable and smart and would win over the voters.

Stan and I trusted Tuttle and Salvatori—more or less. That is, we believed that they truly admired Reagan, liked his toughness, his gritty spirit, his educated conservative philosophy. However, we weren't so certain that they believed in him as a candidate, that Stu Spencer and Bill Roberts, professional managers marinated in a toxic brew of cynicism and doubt, hadn't negatively influenced them. We felt that

Spencer and Roberts didn't see the deeper possibilities in our guy; they were simply mercenaries—hired political operatives moving candidates like chess pieces around a prepackaged board. They didn't think of Reagan in great-man terms. They even exuded a kind of unspoken pessimism about his chances. We had no doubt that they would be very quick to move to George Christopher's side if the tide shifted that way.

In fact, Stan and I sensed that the professionals had already given up and that we were simply going through the motions of a campaign. As if that weren't enough, Tuttle was having a hard time with his health. He suffered from debilitating ulcers, and so he left a lot of the management of the race to Salvatori, which was too bad because Tuttle had a calming influence on Salvatori, who was a hothead.

It's a long time ago now, but some memories remain fresh. I remember precisely that the only facet that the Spencer-Roberts campaign management team really committed to was damage control.

Perhaps they had already come to the conclusion that Reagan was a lost cause, a loose cannon, someone who could master neither the facts nor the rhetoric of professional politics. Maybe they had decided that he needed to be hidden away in the political attic, like a crazy aunt. But of one thing I was certain at the time—they had given up on him. They were convinced that he couldn't be unleashed in a full-blown, full-throated political campaign. He would scramble the facts, become a joke, make them all a laughingstock. And they would forever be tarred with the reputation of the being the smart guys who had thrown it all away backing a no-win conservative candidate. It would ruin them with the Rockefeller Republicans. They would be on the losing side of history.

So it was to be a ghost campaign. They wanted a meek effort that would schedule Reagan to appear in small towns in front of small audiences with diminishing coverage by the frontline media. They were hedging the bet. He would lose of course, but with a maximum of dignity and without shaming the party elders. Then George Christopher would take up the mantle and make the run for governor. They wanted Reagan to take a dive.

Reagan was right. They really didn't trust him.

After the sabbatical in Malibu, Reagan came to see us in our office in the Panoramic Towers in downtown Van Nuys. We were on the top floor of a ten-story building still under construction. The contractors were putting up new drapes, which they'd laid out on the couch. Reagan was on his way to a small town-hall meeting somewhere in the Valley, and he was wearing his usual blue serge suit. He wanted to see where we lived.

We all sat down and rehashed our beach experience—how surprised we all were by the solid connection that we had made and how eager we were to get onto the campaign trail. It was only a quick drive-by visit, a cameo appearance, and after a few moments of pleasantries Reagan got up to go. That's when I spotted it. All the lint from the colorful new drapes had stuck to his suit.

We were horrified—but he was laughing.

"C'mon, fellas, it's just a little lint."

Just a little lint? Showing up like that could seem careless and sloppy to attentive voters—and would generate embarrassing photos with derisive headlines in the next day's newspapers. We called a full-staff alert—secretaries, clerks, researchers, behavioral psychologists, people with impressive degrees from fancy colleges—and put them to work with Scotch tape, removing lint from Reagan's suit. There he was, arms outstretched, laughing his head off, as seven of us battled his lint infestation.

We got him on his way lint-free—our first collaborative effort on his behalf.

Our contract ran from January until June, and so we began to assemble a staff. If we were certain of anything, it was that Stan and

I alone were not enough . . . not even to remove the lint. This was a full-time job calling for a full-time, fully grown, fully trained staff. And not just researchers and historians—we needed someone else, another body to stand at the candidate's side at all times. Stan and I would handle what we could, but we still had teaching jobs. If we divided our time into three zones, one man could always stay with the candidate while the other two were off-watch.

Stan called on his Republican contacts. They recommended Jim Gibson, a PhD candidate in history at Claremont. The head of the department said that he was ideal—mature, level-headed—and he seemed to be a conservative. Jim was a former intelligence officer who had served in Vietnam. He came home from the war and went back to school to get his PhD. He had been a grunt, and he didn't want to serve in the infantry any more.

Jim was in his late twenties and single. A wild sort of character, he regaled us with stories about riding his motorcycle all over the Mekong Delta. One day, it seems, the bike went into a ditch. The motor kept turning, ingesting fertilizer into the engine. And the fertilizer in Vietnam was human excrement. Jim finally managed to drag the bike—and himself—out of the ditch. He tried to clean the bike up, but the smell was ingrained in it, and nothing would ever, ever get it out. He took it back to his base, gagging all the way, and tried to sell it. No takers. He tried giving it away. Still no takers. Then he offered it to the Vietnamese in town. No deal. Finally he took it out in the boonies, took his .45 out and pumped a clip of bullets into it. No one would ever ride that bike again, although smelling like it did, it was unlikely that even the most desperate Viet Cong would have appropriated it.

Jim was a treat. Before he became an intelligence officer, as an infantryman, he'd been wounded. Nothing too bad, but Jim was "salty" as we said in the Navy. One day in a bar in Saigon, he heard some GI giving his opinions about the war; he was against it. The problem wasn't his opinion; a lot of soldiers shared it and, besides, talk was cheap. The problem was that he kept on and on, and just wouldn't shut up. Finally Jim had enough. He cracked a whiskey bottle over the GI's head.

We liked him. Based on these stories and a few others like them, we decided this was the perfect guy to team up with us for the ride to Sacramento.

15

The Circuit

"I'm sorry that they did away with paddles in fraternities."
—RONALD REAGAN ON CAMPUS UNREST

The campaign relaunched in an erratic, emotional state of high spirits (us) and nervous pessimism (almost everyone else). Then, over the course of a few hours in Santa Monica, Reagan, abetted by the people who were supposed to know how to handle these kinds of situations, almost destroyed the whole campaign.

Remember, on day three of Malibu, Stan and I had coached him about remaining cool, about not losing his temper unless it was a carefully calculated outburst designed to make a point.

About a month after the Malibu exercises, Reagan blew up.

Fortunately, I was there. And we were able to turn an imminent disaster into a lesson he would never forget.

The explosion came at a National Negro Republican Assembly, known as the Republican Black Caucus, in Santa Monica. Reagan appeared on the stage with George Christopher. After making their standard openings, the candidates took questions from the audience. The question of Reagan's support for Barry Goldwater in '64 came up, specifically in the context of Goldwater's vote against the Civil Rights

Act. Goldwater's position was that civil rights were a state issue, to be handled on the state level, not imposed by the hammer power of the federal government.

That, in fact, was Reagan's position too, although he wasn't a member of Congress and didn't have a vote on the '64 Civil Rights Act.

Like Goldwater, Reagan always insisted that racial discrimination was wrong and would eventually die a natural death as public opinion turned against it and isolated its practitioners. But, like Goldwater, he was against federal intervention, against the creation of another bureaucracy to handle something that should be handled by the states. He also felt that the rush to protect the rights of some could easily diminish the rights of all Americans. In fact, he had also stated pretty boldly in a speech: "If an individual wants to discriminate against Negroes or others in selling or renting his house, it's his right to do so."

That, Reagan insisted, was the proper position based on the Constitution.

But it was a controversial point. Honorable men might disagree about how ultimately to achieve integration. However, at that time and in that place, the subject of housing discrimination and California politics had reached a critical mass susceptible to the slightest jar.

It had come to that only recently. In 1963, the legislature had passed the Rumford Fair Housing Act. The act provided that landlords could not deny people housing because of ethnicity, religion, sex, marital status, physical handicap, or familial status. Among other things, it outlawed so-called covenants that forbade a property owner to sell his or her house to members of a particular group, which in practice had meant black people or, to a lesser extent, Jews. It was a very unpopular piece of legislation, and was quickly followed by Proposition 14, a proposed amendment to the state constitution that was the public's quick attempt to repeal the law. The Republican-dominated Assembly endorsed the proposition, as did a lot of conservatives, and others much further to the right, including the John Birch Society. Endorsed by real estate agents, it easily got on the ballot—attaining twice the necessary signatures—and was approved by 65 percent of the voters in 1964.

Reagan supported Proposition 14, and Pat Brown opposed it.

Eventually Proposition 14 failed. The California Supreme Court—and, ultimately, the United States Supreme Court—ruled the controversial proposition unconstitutional.

So, as Reagan and Christopher contended for favor before the Black Caucus, these passionate memories didn't lie far from the surface. And although it wasn't widely known, Reagan had bought a parcel of land in 1941 that came with a racially restrictive covenant attached to the deed. The deed wasn't part of the debate, it didn't come up in the Q&A, but Reagan was aware of it—indeed, he had to justify it to himself—and so it had to fuel his sensitivity to the oblique accusations.

In other words, the issues of racism and housing were laden with baggage on all sides.

So during that debate in Santa Monica, when Christopher implied that there was a deeper gist to Reagan's opposition of the Civil Rights Act, he struck a nerve. Reagan, tired and fighting off the flu and the persistent bladder infection, didn't have the opportunity to get into the fine print of his beliefs during the abbreviated question-and-answer period. When challenged by a member of the audience about his opposition to the Civil Rights Act, he said he supported its principles but thought it was bad legislation. He defended Goldwater as a good human being and not a racist.

Then—and you can read the blow-by-blow in Dallek's book—he simply exploded as Christopher continued to needle him, indirectly accusing him of being a racist.

"I resent the implication that there is bigotry in my nature," Reagan shouted. "Don't anyone ever imply that I lack integrity. I'll not stand by and let anyone imply that—in this or any other group."

Then he tossed his 3x5 cards in the air, and with tears of frustration in his eyes he stalked offstage, muttering "I'll get that SOB," (meaning Christopher) and went home. I didn't appreciate fully the extent of his frustration, but I ran after him, and along with Nofziger pleaded with him to come back.

"If you leave now, like this," I said, "you will be branded as unreliable and a racist." He had done the one thing Stan and I had drilled into him not to do on day three in Malibu: He had displayed a petulant temper, and he had looked weak. Fortunately, the TV crews had packed up and gone home before Reagan's outburst, so the damage could be limited.

Nevertheless, if he walked out and didn't return, the audience would conclude that he was angry at black people, rather than at George Christopher. And the word would get out to Reagan's disadvantage.

But that was his hot button, and being called a racist was something he couldn't stand for.

Reagan's own life displayed many instances of courage against bigots. In his senior year in high school, two black football players were denied a night's lodging after a road game; he took them home to sleep in his mother's house. He quit a restricted country club in Hollywood that wouldn't allow him to bring a Jewish guest and joined a Jewish country club. No, prejudice was one accusation he would not tolerate.

He had stormed out not because he was racist but because he wasn't.

So on that night in Santa Monica he stalked off the stage, and there was Bill Roberts weakly giving him the okay to flee the scene. Reagan jumped into the car with Bill Friedman and drove the twenty minutes back to his home. Nofziger had jumped into the car with him.

Reagan fumed all the way home. At the house he was still breathless with rage. "Sons of bitches," he muttered again and again. He was angry at Christopher and his staff. Nofziger was uncertain about whether Reagan did the right thing by stalking off.

I didn't see it that way. Roberts and Nofziger were letting their man crash and burn. I realized that the whole campaign could end right there. I headed for the telephone. I knew the one person Reagan would listen to. I started calling the house . . . but the line was busy. Finally, in a voice somewhere between a scream and a plea, I told the operator that this was an emergency—which, believe me, it was—and ordered her to break into the call. She did, and I got Nancy on the phone. I explained to her what happened and that Ron had to come back. If he didn't, the newspapers would crucify him in the morning, calling him a bigot and a racist. "You must get him to come back," I told her. "They're in the car and should be at your house very soon." I heard the commotion as they came in, lots of talking. Nancy told Ron that I was on the line; she told him what I had said. Roberts and Nofziger were against it. That's when I heard him say the phrase I'd heard once before: "You guys don't trust me, do you?"

That's the moment when the three days in Malibu paid off big time. He knew that somebody did trust him, and know what was in his best interest.

I heard him say, "I'm going back."

He got back in the car. Friedman drove, Nofziger on one side in the back and Roberts on the other. They kept asking, "What are you gonna say?"

Reagan didn't answer. He sat there and went over his thoughts. Before the two men could press some sort of flabby "statement" on him, they arrived at the auditorium, and Reagan jumped out of the car, striding out onto the stage with that big, fat "aw-shucks" grin on his face.

To his great relief, the audience began to stand at his return; they were applauding and cheering, recognizing a true act of courage. Soon, it was a standing ovation.

Lyn Nofziger, Bill Friedman, and me watching the candidate at work at a press event (figures at far left and right unknown).

"I'll answer all of your questions," he said when they finally sat down—and he did. He told them how much he hated prejudice, how he had fought it all his life: in the union, on the job, in his scripts. But he had certain fixed beliefs—the Constitution—and he couldn't ignore the commands of his core beliefs. Otherwise, he wouldn't be Ronald Reagan.

In the end, while they didn't necessarily agree with that stand, they respected it, and he got another standing ovation from the crowd. It proved our point about controlled anger.

The show of temper was, of course, a setback. The *LA Times* ran a Paul Conrad cartoon showing a headless Reagan saying, "I'm looking for the rest of me." Christopher snidely extended his so-called sympathy to Reagan "in this moment of his emotional disturbance." But it didn't get wide currency, and Reagan learned from it, taking our point about keeping calm no matter how the opposition tried to rattle him. The damage was limited, and the lesson was useful.

After the Santa Monica explosions, however, the doubters began to spring up again. He's just "not smart enough or stable enough to be governor," Salvatori told Nofziger. Salvatori was even toying with the idea of drafting former governor Goodwin Knight to run instead of Reagan. Knight had been a very popular presence in Sacramento before Knowland elbowed him out of running for reelection in 1958, opening the door for Pat Brown.

But Holmes Tuttle was a rock. He was for Reagan, period. He calmed Salvatori, who was always running on a short fuse.

To bolster his man, Tuttle took Reagan to the Eldorado Golf Club to play a round with former president Dwight Eisenhower. Custom obligated the former commander-in-chief to remain neutral, but he reportedly told Tuttle after the agreeable match, "I like your boy."

Neutral or not, off the record or not, the widely reported hint of that near-endorsement solidified Reagan's reputation among the weaker supporters within the Kitchen Cabinet.

The campaign stumbled through February without the benefit of any clearly defined chain of command—something that Stan and I thought was essential for victory. The Spencer-Roberts managers laid out the schedules, jammed up the candidate's days with appearances from morning to night, assumed that Reagan would obey his marching orders without complaint. And he did. Reagan was nothing if not a good soldier.

Spencer-Roberts had managed more than fifty campaigns—the great majority successfully—and they seemed to exhibit a certain high level of technical competence. The knowledge of that restrained us from interfering. The staffers knew where the local civic clubs were meeting, how to arrange an invitation, how to manage the nitty-gritty of transportation, whom to greet. They provided the essential food and beverage for an outing, and they alerted the local media to an appearance. It all had the slick patina of professionalism.

However, when Stan and I talked it over, their murky indifference to Reagan himself disturbed us. Even the foot soldiers—the handlers and interns, speechwriters and fetchers—didn't discuss his ideology except to list items that would appeal to a particular group of voters: social programs for elderly citizens; campus protests and crime in the streets for the civic clubs; a jolt of hope and optimism for younger voters; an attack on high taxes for business leaders; and a word of appreciation for our veterans.

And that, as Jim Gibson would tell Curtis Patrick decades later, wasn't the way to go. "For a while," said Jim, "we'd try to anticipate the questions that might be asked—that would arise from the event—and that didn't work out every well because what we thought would *never* come up. So I started going to the events, listening to the questions. Finding out what those people were gonna ask him. And that was a good way to go about it because we got on to a different level than we were on before and that worked."

So we researched, and we polled, and we listened. And we continued to hone his positions and expand his knowledge base, all the while keeping it short and sweet, easy to memorize and easy for his audience to understand.

Gradually, we realized two main themes struck a chord no matter where he spoke: Send the welfare bums back to work—regardless of whether they constituted 5.1 percent of the population or 15.1 percent—and clean up the mess at Berkeley.

Deep down, neither Stu Spencer nor Bill Roberts (nor any of their minions) showed any true, heartfelt commitment to the man, himself—not the way that we felt it.

We were standing right in the midst of it, armed with a limited writ that gave us very little weight in the overall command structure. We had almost no input when it came to strategy. Still, we had plenty to do in the early days: organizing our staff—we had something like 20 to 25 research people working for us, most of them grad student types, getting the black binders organized into a manageable form (and having the information in each black book double-checked by a second researcher), briefing Jim Gibson on his crucial role, which was to stay close to the candidate, at the ready to supply data, and above all to keep close touch with the office when he was out there, on point. Remember, Stan and I didn't trust the many Spencer-Roberts staffers, so Jim was our eyes, our ears, and the guy who made sure our message got through.

Here's an example of how well-tuned our research was: I will quote from just one part of a staff memo dated July 20, 1966, and titled "General Index for Fact Books.

The first item in Volume I is headlined: Agriculture.

And here are the categories it's broken down into:

General Facts
Department of Agriculture: Organization
Agricultural Income
Farm Prices
Government Payments
160-Acre Law
Farm Labor Supply

Migrating Worker's Children: Education and Welfare

Farm Housing

US Food Processors in Mexico

That's just one category, albeit a huge one in the fertile valleys of California. And Reagan memorized every single iota there. Whatever the 160-acre law was (and I confess I have no memory of it), he was, by the time he finished studying our position papers, the greatest expert in the whole state on the 160-acre law. And that kind of mastery of the facts made him unbeatable.

Gibson would have fond memories of those days. "I recall the first time I met him," he says in *Reagan: What Was He Like*, Curtis Patrick's 2011 interviews with some of the surviving Old Guard. "I had been to his campaign headquarters many times, but I hadn't been to his house. The first time I met him I met him at his house. I went to his house because we [the staff] were all meeting there, to leave in one car. And there is a certain amount of professional curiosity about whether the kind of work you've been doing and turning in is going to be acceptable. So, it makes you a little nervous. Generally, I'm not nervous meeting celebrities—certainly *he* was a celebrity, before he decided to go into politics. I guess I have that professional curiosity/nervousness about it. I was just *slightly* nervous. I didn't think—I didn't understand Nancy Reagan's relationship—or I would have *really* been nervous!"

Reagan's energy level was erratic and getting worse. It was that persistent infection. It flared up badly at the end of February. The doctor told him to take it easy, but the candidate wouldn't hear it. He was out there, keeping the schedule, pressing the flesh, fulfilling the promises, being the good soldier, despite the low-grade fever.

After the meltdown, in Santa Monica with the black Republicans, caused partly because he was ill and had been pushed too hard, the brain trust and the Kitchen Cabinet met and decided that they had to ease up. Nancy was getting on the case—pushing for some down time. Reagan had to preserve his energy. Holmes Tuttle told him that he would have to fly. There was no other way to get around the huge state, especially if he was going to campaign in the far north. So they chartered a DC-3, which reporters promptly dubbed The Turkey. The southern part of the state they managed by car and bus, and it made a big difference—having his needs attended to.

No one described the campaign ordeal better than veteran California journalist Bill Boyarsky in *Ronald Reagan, His Life and Rise to the Presidency:*

> *A comfortable Greyhound bus was loaded each morning with sweet rolls and coffee for breakfast; soda, beer, sandwiches, and fried chicken for lunch; and whiskey and gin for the long ride back to headquarters. It was a self-contained home with a lavatory for the long days on the freeways. In the mornings the bus would leave Reagan headquarters and bring the six or seven members of the traveling press, the staff, and the candidate to the first event of the day, which was sometimes a coffee hour with women or a stop at a television station to tape a show for a future viewing. After that would be a noon stop for a speech at a luncheon. In the afternoons there would be a rest stop at a motel. After Reagan's [Santa Monica] blowup over civil rights, the afternoon stop was seldom missed. His nap over, the candidate would rise refreshed for a dinner speech, which would end the day. By 10 p.m. he was usually home in bed.*

Nancy had insisted on the afternoon nap. She was no longer willing to tolerate the relentless pressure on her husband—not when he wasn't well. She was always a ferocious advocate for him. When we showed up at the house one day, she glared at my car and demanded to know where my Reagan bumper sticker was. Thinking on my feet, I gave her a kind of hurt look and said, "Those college kids keep pulling them off." I pointed to some tattered remnants of bumper stickers past to prove my point.

Were they Reagan stickers?

I think so. I certainly hope so.

I saw Nancy flash her steel on another occasion when a writer presented her and Reagan with the cover for a new book. Nancy immediately noticed that someone else's face shared the cover with her Ron. She became visibly angry.

Reagan, ever amiable, defused the situation by saying, "Well, honey, at least I got top billing."

More and more, Nancy included herself on the campaign trips. I preferred going by car. It gave us more privacy. Bill Friedman drove, I rode shotgun, and Reagan sat in the back with Nancy, behind Friedman, so that I could see him, talk to him, brief him on the upcoming event.

For instance, when we were heading to a chamber of commerce, Reagan and I knew he'd have to talk business. I flipped through the books and gave him facts and figures about business in California. By now, thanks to Jim Gibson's research and Stan's polling, we know what the questions would be, and Ron would be ready with the answers.

Nancy at his side, watched in that intense way—a combination of adoration and concern

Reagan took in the briefings brilliantly, absorbing pertinent facts, asking pertinent questions, squinting as he concentrated. I knew that he had it down cold when his face unclenched and he smiled, the squint was gone. He was ready for the next stop. Another thing to remember: Reagan didn't just have an actor's memory. Jim Gibson tells a story in Patrick's book that illustrates just how Reagan's memory worked. Gibson, by the way, had stayed on in Sacramento after Reagan was elected governor. "It may have been June or July 1967 [he told

Patrick]—after Ron had taken office—and he'd gone out of Sacramento to talk to the state agriculture people. The San Joaquin Valley Farmer's Association—that sort of group. And he goes down there and he gives a *knockout speech!*

"And I'm saying to him when we are returning to the Capitol, 'Where'd you get all that information, Governor?' Reagan stopped and thought for a moment and said, *Jesus, Jim, don't you remember? You gave it to me in February!* I didn't even remember researching it. He had gotten ALL of that out of the *Little Black Binder!* He already had the facts. He assimilated them. He was the best speechwriter around. He was *incredible.*"

In March 1966, the polling started to improve—and it wasn't just soft polling, that the voters "liked" Ronald Reagan. The public was starting to *agree* with him. The campus riots had gone on too long, and Watts had burned into their calculations.

When we listened at campaign briefings, the Spencer-Roberts people were starting to get a little more enthusiastic. It wasn't just Reagan's improved technique—the care and rest really heightened his effectiveness—it was a little something we detected in the crowds (more of them now) and the media coverage (more of them, too, and more respectful, finally taking him seriously).

Perhaps the biggest boost of all came from his opponent. George Christopher was a dream campaigner—if you were running against him. He habitually showed up late for events. He looked glum on television, which of course Reagan never did. And if there was one lesson we'd learned from the 1960 presidential race, it was that glum didn't play on TV. The new medium required good looks, optimism, charisma, some brio. And our guy had all of those in spades.

Christopher's organization was a shambles, too, and Stu Spencer's original judgment about him, that there was no growth in the man, seemed borne out by his disorganized appearances.

As Lou Cannon points out in *Governor Reagan: His Rise to Power,* Christopher's chief argument against Reagan was that he couldn't beat Pat Brown. He devoted a good chunk of his television addresses to attacking Reagan's left-wing history. It made Christopher seem petty—and he was violating the GOP's beloved Eleventh Commandment: "Thou shall not speak ill of any fellow Republican." It crippled George Christopher as Reagan quickly adopted the admonition as inviolable biblical text.

No Republican could speak ill of Ronald Reagan without incurring the wrath of the party.

16

On the Road

"A taxpayer is someone who doesn't have to pass a civil service exam to work for the government."

Reagan always broke the ice with a joke. An audience was an audience, he said. Always start with a joke. When he started out in February, Stu Spencer told him to look at the campaign like a stage play in New York. "We're going to go out of town to Visalia and to all the little burgs up in Northern California and try out your act. If you screw it up, only a small number of people will see it. And if it's good, we can keep it."

Reagan understood that.

He also had a rhythm, and he didn't like to be thrown off. Someone jabbing a nasty question in his face threw him off his timing. It took him a long time to get over Christopher's goading in Santa Monica. In fact, he never did get over it. He remembered insults. But he worked on it, and worked on it, and soon he could smile and joke his way through any amount of heckling or ill will. He was growing the thick skin you need if you're going to make it in this business called politics.

In his own way he understood campaigning better than anyone, better than the experts who surrounded him. To him, the whole thing was like show business: You begin with a strong opening, you have a middle, and then you finish strong. He liked that. Rhythm. He got very good at reading the audience. It helped that he was a great raconteur. So he would tell a story or a joke, make a point, and have the audience in the palm of his hand.

"I used to think I was poor. Then they tell me I was needy. They said I was being self-defeating—I wasn't needy, I was culturally deprived. Then they said deprived conjured up a bad image—I was underprivileged. That became overused, and I became disadvantaged. I still don't have a dime, but I do have a great vocabulary."

That was how he saw the world—in yarns that proved a point. A story about a boy who gave his friends a place to sleep when a hotel wouldn't take in black people. A story about a young actor who witnessed a robbery from the window of his apartment, and all he had at hand was an unloaded gun to frighten off the bandit. He said that happened to him and that he was more frightened than the would-be victim. Always there were stories with a message, a meaning. The stories illustrated a point: He wasn't a bigot; he acted despite his fears. Snipers tried to pick the stories apart, tried to prove that they weren't true. But that was never the point. They were true enough for Ronald Reagan. He believed them, and by telling them he made everyone else believe in him.

Of course he did embellish, even invented, a few anecdotes—points that bolstered his case. But they were harmless, not outright lies, just wishful versions of life that had some thread of truth attached to them. Remember, he was the guy who broadcast the story of a ball game from a little thread of tape that came across the wires:

"Cobb is on first, and the fans are yelling for him to steal, and the pitcher looks him back to first and then steps off the rubber and starts his windup, and before he can deliver Cobb is on second base." All he had to work with was the teletype saying: "Cobb stole second." Poetic license, I called it.

There was one particular whopper he persisted in retelling, though, even when proven false with mathematical precision. It was the Dixon High School myth. In his senior year, 1927, Reagan insisted that he had called a penalty against himself when the team was playing Mendota High. It was, supposedly, a crucial penalty, and it cost the team the game, thus demonstrating (without a lot of chest-beating) his virtuous selflessness, even at the cost of victory. I think they call it "humble-bragging" nowadays.

The only problem with this spirited tale was that it wasn't true. One of his biggest admirers, author and journalist Lou Cannon, pointed out that there was only one game in which Reagan was a member of the varsity team, and in that particular contest Dixon lost 24-0. But that didn't stop Reagan from telling the story. Hey! It was a great story, with a moral and everything. That it wasn't strictly true, well, so what? People didn't mind that it wasn't factually correct, they just wanted the right outcome. If it demonstrated a greater truth—the power and resiliency of the American character and spirit—that was good enough, particularly if they trusted the heart behind it. And they would, the more they saw of Reagan.

In mid-March we got a chance to test our effectiveness. We were scheduled to appear before a group of farmers in Salinas Valley where there is always a sharp divide over the water supply. The annual rainfall can't satisfy both the farmers' and the cities' needs, so water has to be diverted from the reservoirs and rivers of Colorado, Oregon, and Mexico. In addition, pumps and reservoirs had to be built to control the flow of water as the snowcaps on the Sierra Nevada Mountains melted. All those books and movies about the epic quest to supply the arid valleys of California were true, it turned out.

As we drove out of Los Angeles County and headed up through the San Fernando Valley, I filled Reagan in on the issue. In those days, it was a three-lane highway. One stoplight in the whole Valley. This was before the freeways. By the time we hit Westwood, it was starting to get a little threadbare, but that was where all the old movie stars had big homes.

The farmers were instinctively wary of politicians, and Reagan needed all his charm to break those weathered frowns. He climbed onto the stage and faced a lot of folded arms. How do you break that ice? Well, with the famous Reagan charm.

"There is no question that we will continue to bring water to the Valley," Reagan began. "One thing I learned pretty early in life—I didn't need to take a bath. But I did need to eat. Food is not a luxury. Farmers are not expendable."

The folded arms broke apart and applauded. He knew how to get through to farmers. He knew it instinctively. That was the part that we had taught him, to trust his instincts. He didn't have to know the rainfall curve or the next pumping project. He had to know what the farmers were worried about.

That's how we campaigned. He had his issues, and he was going to talk about them. Spencer-Roberts didn't always agree. They were following the polling, which said that Californians were interested in tax rates and housing. Reagan was interested in the University of California and the student riots. Spencer tried to tell him that he should tone down the campus stuff. The University of California attacks weren't working. People didn't care that much about the Free Speech Movement or left-wing hero Mario Savio. But Reagan disagreed. He kept pounding the issue, even though Spencer tried to tell him that it wasn't showing up in the polling data.

We were in Fresno in April, and Spencer confronted him. "Ron, the way you keep talking about Berkeley doesn't even show up in the polling data."

He didn't even blink an eye. "It's going to."

Reagan was talking to Spencer, the master of manipulation, and he was dismissing the polling, the study groups, and the think tanks.

Or at least the ones where Spencer was getting his information. He followed his own star and pounded it and pounded it and pounded it, from San Francisco to San Diego, attacking the hippies and radicals and Free Speech activists, calling for a campus clampdown. He didn't have a big TV campaign, he was just one guy running around the state, kicking hell out of the hippies, but pretty soon it started showing up in the polling data. He was bumping up: seven points, nine points, ten points, fifteen points, twenty points. Spencer showed him the numbers, and Reagan simply said, "What did I tell you?"

To his credit, Spencer, who went to have a stellar career, pushing Gerry Ford to the 1976 Republican nomination (to Reagan's detriment) and becoming a trusted adviser to President Reagan during his two terms, took the lesson to heart. Decades later, in a 1994 interview with the *L.A. Times,* he said this about campaigning: "The art comes in making decisions about what your issues will be, and what your basic strategies will be. You can't just sit back, read polling data and say, 'We gotta be for this, we gotta be for that.' People change overnight. The best candidates I've ever seen are people who have a firm belief in something. That's what you have to work off, and it's an instinctive business. You've got to have those political instincts, and that's what makes it an art form."

There are other ways to measure a campaign's effectiveness. Not always tangible—just the mood of a crowd. If they're really excited, you hear a lot of high-pitched chatter as you roll in. And, of course, there's the money. We never left a town without leaving behind pledge cards, literature, buttons, and bumper stickers. The pledge cards were really important. After we left, we had a guy pick up the pledge cards, and pretty soon we had thousands and thousands of people who wanted to work for us and not just to donate money. They wanted to go out, ring doorbells, make phone calls, and drive people to the polls. That's how you build an organization. That's how you get a base.

Bill Friedman, the ex-cop, drove, making certain that whoever was riding shotgun in the passenger seat gave him plenty of room, didn't get too close. Bill had to be able to get at his gun if something went wrong. Not only was Friedman armed, he was extremely protective in every way. He always took the room next to Reagan at the hotels and motels on the road, and he always slept half awake and with the door cracked open so that he could hear activity in the hall.

Friedman was a terrific driver, professional, quick, and reliable. We once got caught in a jam on our way to Santa Cruz, and he swung off the highway and onto side roads and somehow got us there ahead of schedule. Bill always scouted a route ahead of time, always checked traffic with the highway patrol so that they knew we were on the way. I sat beside him, and he chatted away, often talking a lot of nonsense.

Why is this guy so chatty? I wondered more than once . . . and then I realized that he didn't want me to hear Ron and Nancy baby-talking in the back seat.

"I wuv you, Daddy!"

"And I wuv you, Mommy!"

They called each other that in private—or even semi-private, and when they said, "I wuv you," they meant it.

In May, we were in a caravan on our way to a Republican cookout in Santa Barbara, a sleepy coastal town in the west of the state, and everyone was in a pretty good mood because we knew that the food would be good and this was wine country so the refreshments would be plentiful. All the cars had radio hookups to each other, and when I looked ahead and behind I could see the guys in the other cars bouncing up and down and slapping each other silly. They were in hysterics over the baby talk coming out through the radios.

But Ron and Nancy's feelings were too genuine to be silly. This was a real love affair. Every time they got on the stage together, they hugged and gazed into each other's eyes. Every single time. It wasn't

Carefully alert as always, Bill Friedman (foreground, back to the camera) watches Reagan working his magic.

fake. When Reagan had to go to San Francisco and was getting on a train, Nancy would show up at the station with a couple of sandwiches and a piece of fruit in a bag. And they'd kiss like wartime lovers, like he was going away to rescue France and defeat the Nazis singlehandedly. It was deep and authentic. You couldn't witness it and not be moved, not smile at seeing something so simple and so pure.

The security and campaign staff didn't always laugh at Reagan. Often they laughed with him. Once he started to ease up, once the primary campaign started to look—not easy, but doable, say in late April—he was such a ham that he would get on the phone with the car ahead and start telling jokes.

"You know those congressmen who complained about being bugged by the FBI? You'd think they'd be glad someone was listening to them!"

"The Democrats' idea of fighting crime is a suspended sentence."

"Some people try to be so broadminded that they end up shallow."

"When all the cars in Los Angeles are laid end-to-end, it's called a weekend."

"So this husband says to his wife, 'You know, in the six years we've been married, we haven't agreed on a single thing.' And the wife says: 'We've been married for eight years, dear.'"

And, of course, we realized something else: He was testing lines on us. If they worked, he'd use them again when he was in front of the right audience. The audience was Broadway; we were the out-of-town tryout. We were New Haven. If he bombed with us, he either dropped the joke completely, or he'd rework it, tighten it up, tweak the timing, work on the accent. And he'd try it again.

Sometimes he'd slip into dialect—Jewish, Italian, black—and the guys in the other cars howled with laughter. He had great charm.

"So the doctor says to Izzy, 'Listen, I'm going to need a sample of your stool, and your blood, and your urine,' and Izzy hands him his underwear."

Do I need to say that Nancy was nowhere nearby when he told that joke?

In the rural zones of the state, he used stories that he tested in the car to patch bad situations. We were in a small town outside of Riverside, east of Los Angeles, and the crowd was small. Thirty people, all in that stone-faced convince-me mode.

He was ready with a story:

"A minister comes to preach at a rural church, and there's only one worshipper. The minister comes off the pulpit, out into the church, and asks whether he should preach a whole sermon. The worshipper, a farmer, says he wouldn't know about that, being a farmer, but that if he loaded up a truck of hay and took it out into the field and there was only one cow, he knows what he'd do—he'd feed it. Well, the minister took that advice, got back into the pulpit, and preached a fire-and-brimstone sermon.

An hour and half later, he asks the farmer what he thought.

"Well," the farmer says, "like I said, I don't know much about preaching, but I know if I loaded up a truck of hay and took it out into the field and only one cow showed up, I sure as hell wouldn't give her the whole load."

And he told the classic about the small-town preacher who gets around on a bicycle during the Depression. One day, his bike disappears.

He tells his best friend, the local grocer: "I can't believe it. I know everybody in this town. And one of those people, someone who comes to my church every Sunday and listens to my sermons, has stolen my bicycle. I have no idea what to do."

"Well," says the grocer, "here's my advice. This Sunday, why don't you give a sermon on the Ten Commandments. When you get to the Eighth Commandment, 'Thou Shalt Not Steal,' give a long, meaningful look at the congregation. Someone is bound to flinch. And that someone is your bike thief."

"Why, that's excellent advice," the pastor says. "I'll do exactly that."

So Sunday comes, the preacher gets up and launches into his sermon. But when he gets to the Eighth Commandment, he just keeps going, rounds Ninth, slides into Tenth, and the sermon is over.

"What happened?" the grocer says when he runs into the preacher later. "You never did a thing when you were talking about the Eighth Commandment."

"Well," says the pastor sheepishly, "I was going to. But when I got to the Seventh Commandment, 'Thou Shalt Not Commit Adultery,' I remembered where I left the bike."

He also loved the old Pat and Mike jokes. You never hear them anymore because Irish people have ceased to be amusing, slightly exotic immigrants, as they were on the music hall stages of the nineteenth century, and nobody's really come along in the same way to replace them. The thing about them was they were so harmless that an Irishman like Reagan could tell them without running the risk of offending anyone—and people weren't as sensitive about those things in those days anyway.

"So Pat walks into the bar and asks Mike the bartender to pour him a stiff one.

'I just had another ferocious fight with the wife,' says Pat.

'Really,' says Mike, 'How did it end?'

'How did it end?' says Pat. 'It ended with herself coming to me on her hands and knees.'

'You don't say,' says Mike. 'Well, that's a switch. What did she have to say for herself?'

'She said, "Come out from under that bed, you gutless weasel."'

Reagan had a rare gift for putting people at ease in his presence. Then he could unleash the issues, make his campaign points. But he could do it as someone who could see straight through to the end of things.

17

A New Face

Reagan brought along a lot of his Hollywood friends to vouch for him, including Edgar Bergen and George Murphy. Chuck Connors, TV's *The Rifleman*, probably ranked as most popular. Those appearances with the familiar faces gave Reagan a seal of approval with a lot of voters. With the relentless attacks by Christopher about his character, he needed it.

The moderate Republicans came after him over the sensitive issue of the John Birch Society. Rumors swirled that Reagan belonged to the Hollywood branch of the Birch Society along with John Wayne, Adolphe Menjou, Zasu Pitts, newspaper columnist Hedda Hopper, and screenwriter Morrie Ryskind. But Reagan said that it just wasn't true.

The question became how to distance himself from the Birchers without alienating their supporters. Nixon bungled that job in 1962 when he ran for governor and bluntly repudiated the Birch Society; it cost him a lot of votes among the hard-right Republicans who were heavily represented in Southern California. It also cost him a lot of financial support. Reagan didn't want to risk that. When questioned on *Meet the Press*, Reagan said that the FBI had investigated the Birch Society and found nothing subversive about the group. However, he attacked Birch Society founder Robert Welch as "reckless and imprudent."

But Reagan was only willing to go so far. He wasn't willing to tell "a whole segment of the party to go to hell." His solution was to say that if he received support from the John Birch Society it wasn't because he was going over to their side, it was because they were agreeing with him. It worried Spencer-Roberts, but in the end none of it stuck to Reagan.

After the Santa Monica event, the official campaign managers began to display a muted disrespect for the candidate. It was, in some way, natural. If the campaign is failing, the manager doesn't want to get the blame. If it's succeeding, the manager believes the achievement to come from the strength of his magic.

In the case of Spencer-Roberts, Stan and I detected it in the tone of the conversations. Junior staff members referred to the candidate as "Ronnie," a diminutive that he would never tolerate. "Ron" was the acceptable familiar form of address. "Ronnie" was his son's name. If Nancy had ever caught anyone using "Ronnie," there would have been hell to pay.

That disrespect, of course, came from the top: Bill Roberts. He didn't think Reagan was quite ripe. A man who cursed out his opponent, then stalked off the stage—that man was fatally undependable. He should be replaced, they thought, and it was a supposedly altruistic conclusion. They could live without "Ronnie," but the Republican Party had to survive to fight another day.

So the campaign began to cut its losses; that is, they downgraded Reagan's importance. Bill Roberts described the candidate to Bill Boyarsky as intellectually limited: "We decided not to show brilliant knowledge, which he did not have. We decided to operate on the level that he is . . . Joe Doakes running for office."

It wasn't the only demeaning line of attack. Roberts—insensitive to the effects of the urinary infection—complained that Reagan tired easily. "He doesn't hold up well. Give him three or four days of three or four meetings in a row, and he gets real irritable," Roberts told Boyarsky.

In other ways, Spencer-Roberts used the Santa Monica excuse for hedging their bet. They convinced the finance guys that they had to have more control. They couldn't leave the fate of the Republican Party in the hands of two flaky college scientists with incomprehensible theories about influencing the electorate.

They made a deal with Holmes Tuttle: They would remain on the case if they were allowed to have more authority. So they introduced more moderate operatives into the campaign.

Chief among them was Phil Battaglia, hired by Holmes Tuttle as a chief assistant to Bill Roberts, but clearly much more than that. A thirty-one-year-old Los Angeles lawyer with a record of campus activism for moderate Republican causes, Battaglia was on the fast track to make partner at an important L.A. firm. His principal asset, though, was that he was apparently untainted by the struggle between moderate and conservative Republicans. He had supported Senator Thomas Kuchel, a Rockefeller Republican who, as minority whip, had helped shepherd the Civil Rights Act through the Senate. Still, he had the kind of energy and organizational skill that led Lou Cannon to describe him as "a bright young [man] . . .unscarred by internecine party warfare."

As co-manager, Battaglia did give Roberts a larger portion of influence over the conduct of the campaign. Battaglia, a high-voltage manager, put himself in the middle of any dispute. From the first, when he was hired in March, Battaglia didn't approve of our influence—and it was mutual.

He shifted staff and gathered his own army of acolytes—and all the time he took what would have been seen as a liberal position on all the issues. Placing Battaglia in the campaign was a clear attempt to guide the candidate toward a more moderate position in the party. It was a mistake that almost ruined Reagan's political career.

18

Answered Prayer

The Democratic nominee presumptive, Pat Brown, was rooting for Reagan. He was certain he could beat the untested actor in the general election, so he was very interested in the outcome of the Republican primary election.

George Christopher, on the other hand, was an old pro, and the polls showed that he started out with a fifteen-point lead over Brown if they faced each other in November. Reagan and Brown, however, were even, so Brown's team went to work trying to shift Republican voters away from Christopher and over to Reagan. It seemed reasonable. After all, Democrats enjoyed a three-to-two registration advantage in California, and Brown figured that would prove decisive against a raw amateur Republican.

Reagan as governor? "We thought the notion was absurd and rubbed our hands in gleeful anticipation of beating this politically inexperienced, right-wing extremist and aging actor," Brown remembered later. Nor was it an uncommon opinion. When the first whispers began that Reagan might run, Marquis Childs, a national political columnist, wrote, "The polls show Reagan with comparatively little strength."

Brown's team waged a below-the-radar campaign against Christopher, bringing up old discredited charges about implications of illegally price-fixing milk. Christopher owned a dairy, so there was some plausibility in such an accusation, but the price-fixing charges were bogus. At the same time, Christopher's team tried to depict Reagan as a dangerous radical. So the voters had a choice: corrupt versus crazy. In a perverse way, however, the smears worked. A significant number of voters shifted away from Christopher, transferring their allegiance to Reagan, who didn't seem quite as extreme as Christopher seemed shady.

Which was exactly the Brown strategy.

Meanwhile, the war between Reagan and the campus radicals had been building, fueled by Brown and Christopher and the reluctance of Spencer-Roberts to endorse it. Reagan remained convinced that this was a winning issue.

One week after the Santa Monica blowup, he was ready to prove his case that the voters were more concerned with getting rid of campus hooligans than phony issues about his civil rights record. In early March, he scheduled an appearance at Berkeley, the belly of the campus beast.

It was there, at the law school's Boalt Hall, that Reagan confronted the hippies, ultra-liberals, and graduate radicals on Friday, March 11, 1966. There was a lot of anticipation, a lot of concern. The opposition students were organized and angry. Reagan stayed at a motel within walking distance of the campus. In the morning I knocked on his motel door. His muffled voice told me to come in. Reagan was in the shower, and he called out again. "Come on in!"

Reagan was a movie star, someone from a culture of very few inhibitions. The basic requirement of an actor is to put yourself in front of a camera and allow the world to study you, complete. In fact, it's a movie star's duty to seek that kind of attention. So very few actors remain self-conscious about exposing themselves. Not that Reagan lacked modesty—he just wasn't obsessed with his physical privacy.

I had been in the Merchant Marine and the Air Force, so I wasn't exactly bashful. When he called out, I went in. Reagan had to have a briefing for this one. The students were smart and would try to trick him on details. With the briefing cards, we went over the education budgets and the legal arguments against takeovers of public property, the philosophical repugnance of violence, and the reasonable means of making a case.

I told him about Savio, the twenty-three-year-old undergraduate who had a mesmerizing way with a crowd. A former altar boy, he had used the civil rights cause to launch a movement against the Vietnam War, "oppressive" tuition, and any and all authority. He would be there, along with all of his followers, with Reagan cast as the chief villain.

It was, of course, a trap. We had been warned. The student leaders had been preparing for this visit for weeks. They would bring up all the legal arguments to bolster their case, that they were merely exercising their First Amendment right to free speech when they shut down the school. They would legally attack any kind of government crackdown on student rebellion. They would make all the legal arguments against curbing housing bills, reining in welfare rolls, and any other kind of social restriction. The briefing cards contained all the counterarguments—that the administration had a right to protect itself against a student insurgency that threatened its very existence. We had plotted the route he could take to avoid the legal tangle.

The California education system was a thing of pride for liberals like Pat Brown. They had poured more and more money into providing a free college education to the population. What emerged was a huge, ever-expanding educational bureaucracy that supported a hard left-wing constituency that provided a base for opposition to everything from the Vietnam War to alleged police brutality. This is what Reagan was taking on.

I proposed that he take the car directly to the entrance of Boalt Hall and avoid the heckling mob. We could hear the buildup of a crowd outside, the gauntlet he would have to run. But that wasn't Reagan. He came out of the motel and started toward Boalt Hall—walking. Spotters called out that he was on his way. Low hills surrounded the motel, and in the hills—more like rises in the path—students began to rumble as Reagan made the half-mile walk to the hall. They were holding up insulting signs, and the rumble grew louder until it became one long scream that Reagan was a phony and a spokesman for big business and that he was a mouthpiece for the enemy.

He walked in the middle of the road, smiling and nodding, as if these people were fans lining the red carpet on Oscar night. When he approached Boalt Hall, the shouts became deafening. You could almost walk on the sound. Then he put his finger to his lips. That simple gesture had a magical effect. It stopped the roar in its tracks. The students—kids, really—were smiling.

That didn't end the unrest, but during his speech Reagan quoted facts and figures, *accurate* facts and figures, to show that California was helping the poor as much as it could, ten times the load that it carried during the Great Depression. He said that, recently, while skiing in Colorado, he was shocked to find that half the people he met vacationing there were living on California welfare checks. The current laws and the current burden were enough for the taxpayer to bear.

The students were a little taken aback by this Hollywood actor, this first-time candidate, this unproven public figure who had a command of the facts, a sense of humor, such poise in the face of such raw antagonism. The cries from the audience mostly concerned free speech and opposition to the war.

"Of course I believe in free speech," said Reagan. "But once you've committed men to fight and possibly die, then freedom of speech has got to stop short, not give aid and comfort to the enemy."

The campus newspaper, the *Daily Californian,* reported that the room then "exploded." A student leapt to his feet and demanded to know the reason, the exact reason, for fighting in Vietnam. The crowd cheered the question.

Reagan was angry. "There's a blunt word for interfering with a war. In coming together in government, people pledge their collective strength to protect the least individual among them. Right now, that individual is that GI in Vietnam, and we've got to unanimously support him."

The lefties didn't like that answer. But it wasn't crazy, it was reasonable. It was something about which you could argue, and it was apparent that Reagan wasn't a drooling reactionary. He was merely a conservative: afraid of too much government, worried about finding government at the point of a bayonet, seeing clearly the possibility of the corruption of a decent goal, something that could turn against the average citizen.

The civility of his presentation was disarming, even when he defended his position on the 1964 Civil Rights Act. "I have always been heart and soul for the goals of the act . . . [however] I seriously question its methods." The students detected the unmistakable aura of sympathy in him. Ronald Reagan was not a monster.

The students still didn't like him, but they saw a human side, and they couldn't just dismiss him as a robotic arm of "the man." It was a standoff, but the confrontation was far from over.

19

A Distraction

Stan and Jim and I and the rest of BASICO didn't exist—not as far as the campaign managers were concerned. It was in the long-term interest of the campaign to deny our purpose. They couldn't very well deny our physical presence; we were noticeable, hanging close to the candidate, consulting with Reagan on his notes, polishing his speeches, and working on the schedule. It was a fairly intimate relationship, and there were no minders telling us what to do. Anyone studying the way we operated could see that we were independent, answerable only to Ron.

But it was the job of the newspaper reporters to notice just such an unusual arrangement. The media guys saw that we had an important role in the overall operation, but it was vague and undefined. They saw us on buses, cars, and the plane to San Francisco, but, when they tried to get us to describe our exact role, we said that we were just another couple of members of the staff. We maintained our mysterious distance from the probing eyes and ears of the press. Which made them uneasy and more determined to crack our mission. Unlike some media hogs on the bus, we were comfortable living in that shadow.

Then we became an issue.

By late spring, newspapers and magazines began running stories and even editorials about the two weird behavioral scientists who

Reagan holding a press Q&A session at an airport. That's the back of Bill Friedman's head to the right of Reagan.

had entered the race. The *San Francisco Chronicle* quoted Democratic sources who claimed that we were "twisting public opinion" for the sake of "mass manipulation." Stories showed up in the *Sacramento Bee* and the *New York Times* that Reagan was using mind-altering ruses to fool the public. Whatever tricks could be played on the subconscious minds of the voters—exploiting their worst fears about Communism, riots in the streets, out-of-control hippies, government's reckless spending—were ascribed to the influence of the two Frankenstein sorcerers practicing their dark arts with the candidate. The new age of Madison Avenue subliminal mind-benders had dawned. Subconscious suggestions and brainwashing were frightening but not inconceivable concepts to the public.

Eugene Wyman, the Democratic national committeeman for California, charged that the Reagan campaign was using behavioral scientists "to exploit public opinion on campaign issues." He meant us. State Republican vice chairman James W. Halley shot back: "Look who's talking." Then he added, "What's wrong with finding out by modern means why people don't like them?" He was referring, of course, to the Democrats.

Nevertheless, Wyman named us—"Dr. Stanley Plog of the UCLA faculty and Dr. Kenneth Holden of the State College in the San Fernando Valley"—and accused us of fiendishly rooting out "the hidden fear and prejudice of the people" to manipulate the masses. The *Saturday Evening Post* even mentioned us, suggesting that we introduced a "newfangled, scientifically enhanced" evil threat into American politics. It all sounded so ominous, so evil, so foreign. According to the *Chronicle,* it was our influence that caused Reagan to support the repeal of the Fair Housing Act. Now that was a stretch.

When our names became public, Stan and I came under professional pressure to quit the campaign. Both of our academic communities abhorred the notion of two colleagues involving themselves in something as crass as politics—meaning Republican politics. We were supposed to remain aloof, only theoretically engaged in life outside of the ivy tower. Controversy, meaning real-world problems, was beneath us. Unless, of course, we could find something liberal to support. The hypocrisy was intolerable.

Stan came under fire first. One of his so-called well-meaning colleagues pulled him aside and told him in utter confidence that he would have to give up one or the other, the teaching post or the political activity for the Republican Party. I was approached a day or so later, but it was the same threat. Give up politics or lose your job at the university.

Stan later told me how he ran afoul of the same Orwellian concept of "academic freedom." It started with his research on the Watts riots. "My mission," said Stan, "was to focus on understanding community social problems. We applied for and quickly got a large federal grant to study the causes and cures. I put out a call to all the top people in the departments of psychology, sociology, economics, political science, and public affairs at UCLA. The team assembled quickly.

"Everything went smoothly for probably eight months except that I was attacked in the newspapers of the Far Left, stating that I was a 'capitalist running-dog lackey who used poor black people as research subjects to exert control over them,' and by the Far Right for using government funds to support the cause of rioting blacks.

"Other than that, I worked several months without incident when, unknown to me, a revolt started behind my back. The *New York Times* did a story mentioning the work Ken and I were doing for the Reagan campaign. The UCLA faculty was upset. Dr. Werner Hirsch, my boss at the Institute of Government and Public Affairs, called me to confront me around August 1966, and gave me the dictum that I either had to drop the Reagan campaign or leave the Institute. I was totally caught off guard and shocked at the demand. I told him he had no right to make that demand; I had done nothing wrong and was on top of my assignment. The academics said that black leadership and the ACLU hated Reagan so much they would make a big stink about the project being led by a John Birch supporter (which is how they characterized my support of Reagan). I confronted Hirsch with the question about whether he realized this was a question of academic freedom and that I, as a conservative, also had rights.

"In the end, I would win. The university review committee would have to support me or there would be a big stink in the press and I would sue. But I was so disgusted, I told Hirsch I would make his job easier—I would resign immediately and devote myself full-time to my fledgling company. Now, I could devote more effort to the Reagan campaign."

That, of course, was the unintentional gift of the Left to the rest of us: The more obnoxious they were, the more they advanced the cause of Ronald Reagan and those of us who despised them and, to quote Orwell, their "smelly little orthodoxies."

But the exposure did bother us. It damaged our effectiveness, and it could have compromised us with Reagan. We talked it over with him, and he took it in stride. He told us not to worry about it, just keep doing our job.

Spencer and Roberts, however, didn't like the attention one bit. Battaglia hated it. So a new campaign began: one of denigrating our work. The star newspaper reporters got private, off-the-record, sometimes *on*-the-record briefings by Stu Spencer, Bill Roberts, or Phil Battaglia, letting them in on the dirty little secret: that we were brought in to work with Reagan during the desperate hours after the initial press conference blunders, when the campaign hung in the balance. Our job was to restore Reagan's confidence. But now, that need was over. We were superfluous.

Still, we received credit for some influence. David S. Broder, national correspondent for the *Washington Post*, noted Reagan's wide range of literary allusions, which included such names in his speeches as de Tocqueville and John Stuart Mill, "a sort of wisdom-by-association technique also used by President Kennedy."

That was our hidden hand at work.

In a sense, this attempt to diminish our role acted as a kind of compliment. The Democrats were glad to use us as bogeymen to frighten the electorate, and the press enjoyed making fun of us as counterfeit wizards. But the subtle and not-so-subtle muggings by

Spencer-Roberts, the very guys who hired us, proved hard to take. Not so much Stu Spencer—because he wasn't around as much—but Roberts and Battaglia had become our openly declared enemies. They hung over us like a sulfuric cloud. We were convinced that it was the galling fact that the candidate was gaining traction with the voters that Roberts and Battaglia couldn't stand.

It was confusing for them as well. At the same time that we began to get attention, they began to recognize the possibility of a primary victory, and the campaign began to take on new urgency and therefore life.

Battaglia recruited an army of his own to perform all the advance work, getting tickets, arranging speeches, making hotel reservations, seeing to transportation and the comfort of the press—all the details missing from the operation when we first encountered it.

So, we were happy about that. It began to feel like a winning campaign.

That was a good thing. But we found the behavior of Battaglia's army . . . disconcerting.

Their shenanigans put us out; we read it as a kind of boyish and silly enthusiasm. But we thought that maybe we were overreacting, maybe we were prejudiced by our inherent dislike of Battaglia and Roberts. But we couldn't not be aware of the giggling late-night parties in hotel rooms, the guys running through the hallways, yelling and half-naked. It seemed immature, sure, but not outright threatening.

It would turn out to be politically very dangerous to Ronald Reagan—but that came later, when he was already ensconced in the governor's mansion in Sacramento. In the meantime, Battaglia's people let us know we were outsiders, not on the same team. That was fine by us. We had the confidence of the only one who counted.

Meanwhile, Reagan had gotten his sea legs. He no longer sounded timid about his beliefs, he was no longer was shy about his message. He had even developed a kind of campaign swagger.

He had absorbed the lessons of Malibu.

On Thursday, May 12, in what was billed as the "major primary event in Northern California," a "star-spangled rally" of about five thousand people jammed into the Cow Palace on the outskirts of San Francisco for a $7.50 pre-speech box lunch of fried chicken, apple pie, and political hot pepper. There, under the world's largest American flag that swept from one end of the stage to the other (94 feet by 144 feet), with great swaths of red, white, and blue bunting stretched around the arena, Chuck Connors introduced "a man in a state that needs a man." Don DeFore (of *The Adventures of Ozzie and Harriet* and *Hazel*) and Buddy Ebsen had already trod the boards, promoting their friend, and now they stood with everyone else to applaud and cheer the roof down.

In came Ron and Nancy, holding hands, smiling, looking like they'd already won the race. As Nancy withdrew to her seat, Reagan stood before the whooping crowd with that little glint of danger in his eyes.

There are moments when the world seems to shift, when something powerful takes over and nothing will ever be the same again. Such a moment came at the Cow Palace on that night in May when Ronald Reagan declared war on the administration of the entire university system in California. His set his sights on Clark Kerr, the enabler of the Free Speech Movement, the coddler of kids smoking marijuana, the liberal administrator who tolerated, encouraged, and turned a blind eye to what Reagan called "the morality gap." Nothing short of Kerr's dismissal would satisfy the candidate, he said, and the crowd hooted in agreement.

"There is a leadership and a morality and a decency gap in Sacramento," Reagan declared. "There is no better illustration of that than what has been perpetuated on the Berkeley campus at the University of California where a small minority of beatniks, radicals, and filthy speech advocates have brought such shame to and such a loss of confidence in a great university that applications for enrollment were down 21 percent this year and expected to decline even further next year."

What raised his ire was a recent dance held at Harmon Gymnasium by the Vietnam Day Committee on March 25. According to Reagan, who had seen excerpts of a report on the dance from a State Senate committee, the campus "has become a rallying point for Communists and a center of sexual misconduct." Reagan said that there were incidents at the dance that were "so bad . . . so contrary to our standards of human behavior that I cannot recite them to you in detail."

"The report tells us," he continued, "that many of those attending were clearly of high school age. The hall was dark except for the light from two movie screens [where] the nude torsos of men and women were portrayed, from time to time in suggestive positions and movements. Three rock and roll bands played simultaneously. The smell of marijuana was thick. There were signs that some of those present had taken dope. There were indications of other happenings that cannot be mentioned here. . . . The dance was only called to halt when janitors finally cut off the power. And this is certainly not the only sign of a leadership gap on the campus."

Here, bound together in a report on the one event, were all the grievances against the counterculture. The attacks on the Vietnam War, the free-speech and free-love movements, the use of drugs, and the general unchecked "abandon" by California youth. Reagan called for an investigation by the State Legislature of the "filthy speech movement."

Until that moment, the student movements that had run riot around the state had cowed California politicians, both liberal and conservative. But Reagan issued a clarion call to arms. He openly was taking on the youth movement, the anti-war, anti-establishment, anti-religion, anti-authoritarian . . . anti-anything surge. It was exactly the right moment to strike. Soft, ethereal speeches about ideology and philosophical principles fell in the face of specific, hard assaults on the complacency of college presidents, impotent chancellors, bureaucratic apathy, handcuffed police, strangled media, overage children, and left-leaning faculty.

Ronald Reagan was serious, and it showed.

20

"I Am Not a Politician!"

George Christopher didn't know what hit him.

Suddenly, Ronald Reagan was campaigning like an old pro. He got up before a crowd—any crowd, north, south, east, west, it didn't matter—and brought up his argument about "the filthy speech movement." The audience took his side, swept away by his confidence and conviction. He seemed in complete control. Even the hecklers were abashed to be tackling such a patently decent man.

In San Diego, a man yelled out that Reagan was a lousy actor.

"Hey! That's why I'm changing jobs," Reagan shot back. That's how to handle it.

They loved it when he turned the tables and showed that underlying touch of wit and humor. He was always in such a good mood, even when he went after the colleges. He kept it up in the cars as we traveled up and down the valleys, telling jokes over the intercom:

"Government's view of the economy could be summed up in a few short phrases: If it moves, tax it. If it keeps moving regulate it. If it stops moving, subsidize it."

He couldn't have been happier now that he had his own audience, now that he proved his case against his own doubting backers. It was amazing to watch the audiences come over to his side. They

The campaign team at San Diego's famous Hotel del Coronado. From the left, one of Bill Roberts's minions, me, another minion (who showed up and shoved us into the back, which is where we preferred to be, anyway), Stan, Bill Friedman, Lyn Nofziger, and the candidate himself. Roberts's men came out of nowhere, and I never saw them again.

just couldn't attach anything mean to Reagan, not the good guy in the movies. He had a golden touch. The "filthy speech movement" might have sounded cranky coming from someone else—but not from him. You could disagree with him, but you couldn't hate him for it.

George Christopher too slowly understood that about Reagan. His counterattacks were calculated to get some traction, but they didn't stick.

Bill Boyarsky, in *Ronald Reagan: His Life and Rise to the Presidency*, called Christopher's campaign a disaster. "He was a bulky, rough-featured man with two successful terms as mayor of San Francisco behind him, but he was little known in Southern California, and he was a poor campaigner for the age of television. He was effective and even dominating in a small group, but he had little feeling for the language, and in speeches he became entangled in such sentences as: 'I am cognizant of two philosophical thoughts which perhaps pertain to this election.'"

Gimme a *break!* It was a chore to listen to that construction, and he hadn't even said anything yet! As the campaign wound down, Christopher knew he was flubbing it. In a desperate move to salvage the race, he attempted to depict Reagan as mentally unstable (always back to the Santa Monica episode in which the candidate flung down his notes and fled the scene). Christopher said that you couldn't trust such a man in the governor's mansion. "Mr. Reagan, of course, has been ill, and I extend my sympathy in this moment of his emotional disturbance."

Reagan shook off the condescending insult and dealt with the charges of extremism and "conventionality" with humor. "I can't be an extremist and conventional at the same time. You can't have it both ways," he told reporters.

He jovially defended his sometimes erratic behavior claiming this whole business of politics was new to him. In the beginning, he joked, he mistakenly confused it with show business, in which he went out on tour and eventually it ended. "In my mind, I had agreed to something that would only last until November. [Then it dawned on me] Wait a minute! If I win this damn thing I'm out of show business! I'm in politics!" That's from Morris's book *Dutch,* so I can't vouch for its literal truth, but it sounds like the Reagan I knew.

The truth is that he was a terrific politician. He held in his hand his campaign "cheat" cards, our pocket-size cardboard notes, so that he could glance down at the gist of his positions in front of him. They were still small enough to keep out of sight. Our job was to provide the up-to-date, right information, statistics on jobs, taxes, crime, and so on. The candidate transformed our raw data into his own music.

By now Phil Battaglia had become campaign chairman. As the smell of panic and defeat faded from the scene, he tried to bury us, tried to bump us from schedules and events. He was operating under the direction of Bill Roberts, who wanted to shed us completely from the campaign after the primary. We were a handicap, according to the managers. Reagan had another opinion, and in a number of private sessions the three of us reminisced about the days in Malibu when the whole thing had slowed down and we could sit in beach chairs and sip iced tea and stare at the Pacific in blissful silence. It was that intimacy—plus the contract under which we still operated—that kept Battaglia and his army at bay.

But we were all still out there, on the hustings, surrounded by more and more reporters. The quiet interludes were growing even more rare.

Van Nuys is a mid-sized town halfway between Los Angeles and Simi Valley. Reagan could always count on drawing a decent crowd at a rally at a local auditorium there. The citizens weren't at all convinced about their own politics, nor were they at all enthusiastic about the arguments, but they were always civil. They listened to Reagan's anti-government speeches with polite attention.

It was late May, and the primary election lay only a week or so away. Reagan had gotten his second wind. His urinary infection was under control, so he didn't tire so quickly. "I am not a politician," he told the citizens of Van Nuys, according to Lou Cannon. "I am an ordinary citizen with a deep-seated belief that much of what troubles us has been brought about by politicians; and it's high time that more ordinary citizens brought the fresh air of common-sense thinking to bear on these problems."

The audience sat there and applauded, and some of them actually reconsidered all of the unnecessary regulations on and government intrusion in their lives. They thought about it. But even more important, they reconsidered this old actor with his combination of sincerity, humor, and convictions.

June 7 was a partly cloudy day and a bright sunny day, it was a rainy day and a dry day. California is a big state, and the weather varied from Sacramento to San Diego. Turnout for the primary was heavy.

Christopher learned the hard way that he had been taken to the woodshed. The man he had dismissed as a dilettante and a broken-down actor beat him by more than two-to-one. Reagan received 64.6 percent of the vote (1,417,623) to his opponent's meager 30.8 percent (675,683.) It was an eye-opening victory. Up and down the line, Reagan was proven right, as were we, BASICO, and all the behavioral psychologists who had worked day and night on the campaign.

In the governor's mansion in Sacramento, Pat Brown, who had hammered Yorty by close to 900,000 votes, misread the results. He saw George Christopher's defeat as his own victory. Now all he had to do was crush a washed-up actor in the general election.

It wasn't the last time that he—or a lot of other people—underestimated Ronald Reagan.

21

New Agreement

"That's not our agreement!"

"Well, there's a new agreement."

We were in Henry Salvatori's office in downtown Los Angeles, Stan and I, and fighting with him again. Our contract to assist Reagan, which we had made with Salvatori, had expired. The primary was over, and we had won the battle. Now it was time to finish the war and take on Pat Brown. Salvatori wanted us to reenlist and stay for the general election, with one new condition: We had to report to Roberts.

Stan had warned me. He said it would come to this and that maybe we would have to bend. I was thinking, *Here we go again!* How many times do we have to go through this? This is our third go-round with Salvatori, and it's beginning to feel familiar, sort of like Jake LaMotta and Sugar Ray Robinson. By now, everybody knew the other guy's moves.

Our negotiating sessions played out like this: We ask for something. Salvatori says no. Then he yells at us. Then Stan tries to restrain me. I yell back.

"Not in a million years!" I tell Salvatori.

The man across the desk was wearing a five-hundred-dollar handmade suit, a bespoke silk shirt, and he glittered with diamond cufflinks and a two-thousand-dollar platinum wristwatch. Gold rings encircled the cracked, callused hands of an old oil-field roughneck. The fingers that glittered with precious metal were broken and bent like a beat-up oil shaft, the muck so deeply embedded within the cracks of his hands that it was impossible to tell where the stains began and the skin ended under the platinum timepiece. When he said what he said, with his stone fist clenched on top of the desk, it was hard to imagine him backing down.

"You're going to sign."

If I wasn't made of the same tested steel of the man across the desk, neither was I made of putty. No, we were *not* going to sign. Putting Roberts and Battaglia in charge was exactly what we were trying to avoid in the first place. I was building a head of steam. Those two guys were salmonella, and we weren't going to swallow that crap. Once those boys got between us and the candidate, we were effectively washed up. We didn't like them; they didn't like us. But even more important, they didn't believe in us and what we were trying to do. To them, behavioral science was voodoo, and we were evil shamans.

"There is no new agreement if we don't agree to it, and I can tell you now, Mr. Salvatori, we're not signing on to serve under Bill Roberts."

"You had it your way under the first contract, son. However, this is a new contract. This is a new agreement."

"Not if we don't sign."

It's a strange thing to engage in a throwdown with a man of Salvatori's hard character and estimable grit. I admired him.

"Listen, fellas, I appreciate what you've done," he said. "Ron appreciates what you've done. But now we're entering the grown-up race. This isn't just a primary; this is a formal, serious, full-blown bid to be the next governor. If you want to ride this train to the end, you'll sign the deal."

"You don't seem to get it, Mr. Salvatori. We are not going to sign on under those conditions."

That got a little under his thick skin. "Well, there's a little some-thing you don't understand: I sign the checks!" Now he's starting to yell.

Stan claimed that, at that moment, I began to raise my voice.

"Let me tell you what you can do with your checks!"

That's not the way I remember it. I was emphatic, yes. But yelling? I don't believe that I raised my voice beyond the ordinary range of conviction. It's true that I was having a tough time making Salvatori see our position, which was that reporting to Roberts would fatally compromise our whole effort. It would render us useless. We'd seen what had happened to the minions who had to report to Roberts. They became deferential little fawners, or they were chopped off.

The Roberts-Battaglia staff, apart from us, became a private club. And it wasn't a club Stan or I wanted to belong to. We kept seeing these light-footed characters floating through hotel lobbies on per-sonal missions, chasing each other through corridors, giggling and squirting water pistols at each other on the airplane, sneaking out of each other's rooms in the middle of the night. Stan and I couldn't prove anything definite about what was going on, but it was pretty clear—and it wasn't our cup of tea. We weren't going to work for Rob-erts, Battaglia, or any of their other fancy helpers.

"That's a deal breaker, Mr. Salvatori."

Salvatori came from behind his desk and started pacing the office—opening and clenching those uncompromising fists—unable or unwilling to see our point.

It was a tricky moment. We couldn't appeal our case to the candi-date himself because Reagan was incapable of firing anyone person-ally. He left the dirty work to people like Salvatori. We couldn't raise some of the chief objections to Battaglia and his corps because they were based on cultural disapproval. The young men in Roberts-Batta-glia's club were, to us, and later when they were exposed, a danger to Ronald Reagan's career. I had my own reservations about overt sexual misconduct, as it was then characterized, but that wasn't why I was taking such a strong stand.

So I pointed out to Salvatori, as calmly as I could, the reasons it wasn't possible to work in such an environment. Battaglia's men were a close-knit group, I said, and a Machiavellian fog hung over the campaign as the staff members plotted against one another, sought favor and privilege with gossipy knifings, and plotted in the wings as Principe Battaglia remained offstage, enjoying the bloodbath but keeping his hands clean.

Tuttle and Salvatori were the original Reagan backers. They had put the ship in the water, so to speak, then rescued the campaign after Reagan kicked a hole in the boat (to test the metaphor), but it was we, Plog and Holden, who plugged up that hole in Malibu. It was Plog and Holden who kept Reagan afloat when almost everyone else was ready to jump ship.

Salvatori relented. To his credit, Salvatori recognized our contribution. Also to his credit, he was a tough, opinionated guy who could change his mind, even in the midst of a confrontation where other men might just become more adamant.

The hands unclenched. He was quiet for a moment, looking me up and down.

"So you won't work under Roberts?"

"That's the deal."

He nodded, he understood. Whether he understood the full range of our complaints, we never knew—but it was enough. Roberts, of course, wasn't happy. From there until the general election, he gave us dirty looks, his cigarette dangling below his curled lip.

But we didn't care. We felt the same contempt for him that he did for us—and continued to report only to Salvatori and Reagan.

After the primary there came a brief lull in which the campaign team debated tactics for the big race. It helped that some of

George Christopher's big backers joined us—Justin Dart, Leonard Firestone—along with their big money. But as in all such rough blendings, it wasn't all clear sailing. Dart, the pharmaceutical tycoon, was an unreserved firebrand and still a little bitter about Christopher's defeat. He remained cool about Reagan's chances and in fact was quoted as saying that the candidate "didn't have a snowball's chance in hell" of beating Pat Brown. Nevertheless, he tried to take over the campaign anyway, arguing that Reagan should lay low and let the governor beat himself.

It wasn't dissimilar to the ideas of Spencer-Roberts, who also wanted Reagan to play defense. They argued that the more aggressive stands on social issues hurt Reagan among moderates. They also wanted to avoid direct confrontation with reporters and having the candidate take questions from the audience at a rally. Reagan was either too glib or too radical, Roberts said.

Stan and I got into some heated conversations with him over that. Reagan was great, even when he hesitated or repeated himself—which wasn't often because our intense briefings prepared him for the toughest questions. He still came out ahead. Everyone thought him authentic and sincere.

Roberts insisted that the polls weren't reflecting a growing popularity. We argued that it was a quirk in the polls. A lot of voters didn't want to admit that they supported a candidate depicted in the press as a failed actor with a low IQ even if they agreed privately with his positions. So we tried a statewide poll with the technique of blind answers, using an innovation of Stan's devising. To collect an unpolluted sample of voter thinking, he had people cast their preference on a ballot, then drop the ballot in a box that the pollster wore on his back. Having the pollster face away, unable to see the ballot, reassured the voter of the secrecy of the vote. That, in turn, gave a much more accurate picture of public opinion.

Using this method, our polls showed Reagan coming out way ahead.

I predicted that he'd win by a million votes.

July was quiet. Reagan had minor surgery to remove some kidney stones. It relieved him of a lot of pain, and the rest helped restore his spirits. By August, we plunged back into the campaign with baby-bright gusto. Pat Brown had been attacking Reagan as a lightweight, and we weren't doing much to counter it.

I had the idea of putting Reagan on stage for a TV appearance flanked by two conservative-leaning Nobel laureates who would endorse the candidate's policies, thus lending gravitas to his candidacy. I still think it was a good idea. Reagan thought so at the time. Roberts dismissed it out of hand.

In early September, after Labor Day, the media coverage started to heat up. The reporters from the East—the *New York Times, Washington Post, Wall Street Journal, Newsweek*—were joining the campaign, climbing into the Reagan bus headed to the small stops in the San Fernando Valley. They all wanted face time with the candidate. Reagan stood up in the front of the bus, the perfect host, entertaining all with his brogue, as Pat and Mike (well, just Pat this time, unless the priest's name is Father Mike) made yet another appearance:

"So Pat, a little the worse for the whiskey, goes into the confessional, and the priest waits to hear from him, but there's nothing but silence from the other side. Finally, the priest knocks on the window, but still nothing. Again, the priest taps the confessional window, and finally Pat replies: 'Yer wastin' yer time, there's no paper on this side, either.'"

He had a soothing effect on the people around him, and when we got to Covina or Santa Barbara or anywhere we had a crowd, Reagan was comfortably at home. "I'm not a politician," he'd tell them. "I'm an ordinary citizen with a deep-seated belief that much of what troubles us has been brought about by politicians."

It was his theme, one that Stan and I promoted, folksy common sense, and it worked.

Meanwhile, Pat Brown, who had been so certain of what to do when Richard Nixon was the opponent four years ago, was going about things the wrong way, wallowing in the indecision that would undo him. He didn't know whether to attack Reagan or ignore him. So he ran a low-key campaign. He called the challenger a dangerous right-wing extremist, while also calling him an amiable lightweight thinker. We went among the reporters and passed along our own judgment, that calling Reagan both constituted a "false duality, a cognitive dissonance." In other, non-psychology words, you can't have your cake and eat it, too. You can't have it both ways.

Finally, when his poll numbers began to slip, Brown panicked and made a TV ad in which he told a group of school children that an actor, John Wilkes Booth, had killed Abraham Lincoln. It was a disaster. The ad was tasteless and inappropriate. And it was stupid. After all, everyone in California, especially in the L.A. area, either knew someone who was an actor, or wanted to be an actor, or had a screenplay in a desk drawer. Or wanted to direct. The polling began to move in Reagan's direction.

Then in October, came a bombshell: Salvatori called a meeting and said that Spencer-Roberts had a mole in the Brown camp and that this mole told them that Brown's people were about to unleash a series of newspaper ads making accusations of sexual misconduct on our side.

Spencer and Roberts questioned Reagan about his behavior. He swore that he had no secrets from Nancy, that he was faithful. So it wasn't him, which was the main thing.

The ad campaign never happened because the behavior mentioned didn't involve the candidate. It reportedly smeared staff members, presumably Battaglia's people, and it was pulled because Brown's campaign decided that because it wasn't about Reagan it probably wouldn't affect the outcome anyway.

22

And . . . Cut!

In his way, Reagan was a cautious man. He didn't necessarily believe it when told that the check was in the mail. He'd had his share of disappointments in that department. When he actually got the check, felt it in his hands, had tactile feedback, he was only partly convinced. He felt secure only when the check had cleared and he had the cash in hand.

So telling Reagan in those last weeks and hours of the campaign that he was going to win—and that it was probably going to be by a landslide—didn't provide great comfort. The check was still in the mail.

He continued to ride the buses and cars and rickety old DC-3 airplane, going up and down California, telling the voters that he had a single great virtue above all others: his lack of experience. Just look at the other guy, he said, pointing to Pat Brown. Look what his experience had wrought.

On Wednesday, November 2, six days before the general election, we went north. The staff calculated that the south was safely in the bag. But San Francisco and Oakland were still in play; at least that was the thinking. We got on board The Turkey—that decrepit old DC-3—and flew up to Napa Valley.

It was harvest season, and we had to make our way out to Santa Rosa and Vacaville where Reagan delivered his standard appeal: his status as a "civilian" in a political war whom they could trust to manage the government fairly. He went through crowds with a professional ease. He touched hands, rather than shaking them. It was a trick of campaign efficiency that he had learned from an old Kennedy staff member. Kennedy didn't shake hands when he could help it, Reagan was told. You could touch two hundred hands in the same time that you shook twenty—and you wouldn't have to soak your bruised hands at the end of the day, like a fighter coming off fifteen rounds. So Reagan went through Fairfield and Concord, touching the hands of the voters.

In San Francisco, while staying at the Fairmont Hotel, we went out to Chinatown for dinner. The mood was one of quiet confidence. We took a slow walk through the streets afterward, mellowed by the fortunes that Nofziger had planted in our cookies: "Reagan will win by 500,000 votes."

I had predicted a million-vote landslide. But earning a reputation as a psychologist who argued with fortune cookie predictions struck me as a bad career move. So I kept my mouth shut for once. It was a sweet moment, and as we strolled contemplatively we saw that some Chinese-American citizens flashed Reagan buttons. Nofziger made a joke about how an hour later he'd probably want another candidate. We groaned.

But Reagan was in such a good mood. The next day as we drove down to San Mateo, he grabbed the car's microphone:

"Two Frenchmen are walking down the street, and they suddenly stop. One says, 'Quick, hide. It's my wife *and* my mistress!'

"The other Frenchman says, 'I was just going to say the same thing!'"

A couple of times we allowed reporters in the car to witness the briefings and the tactical conversations with Reagan, a highly confidential activity until then. They always came away impressed by the high quality of the exchanges.

It had all come together in Malibu, working together. We trusted each other. We flew someplace or drove somewhere, talking all the time. We lost track of everything except the mission, following him into the bathroom, giving him three alternative positions about, say, the farm situation, the eternal irrigation problem, the right-to-work implications. He took it all in, delivering it back to an audience with passion, always sounding fresh and reasonable.

Brown, in those last days before the vote, had fallen into a dark funk. He knew that the race had slipped away. It was drummed home when he asked to tour a riot-ravaged area in a black section of San Francisco, and was told to stay away. Even the black leaders who once had supported him now spurned him. Slumped in the back of his plane, *The Grizzly II,* Brown accepted defeat. He had become yesterday's man.

On that last lap of the race, Reagan was ... I hesitate to say "flying," but he was certainly up. The only thing that got him a little down was the Brown campaign, which continued the same tactics of personal demolition that had succeeded on Nixon. But we reminded him of the chess game, the long game.

One particularly wacky event took place near the very end. During one stop in San Francisco, one of Brown's people was tape-recording Reagan's speech, which usually ended when he said that his intention was "to put out the prairie fire" on the campuses. As a way of mocking him, she whipped out a water pistol, to quench "the prairie fire." She actually had a bunch of water pistols and handed them out to the reporters on the press bus.

And so, boys being boys, the reporters spent the rest of the day squirting each other. On the plane back to Los Angeles, somewhere high over central California, the water fight escalated as gin replaced the water. Guys ran up and down the aisles, squirting gin at each other—a scandalous waste of perfectly good gin, I say.

Then one of the reporters pulled out a trumpet and played the "Charge!" bugle call over and over. I still have no idea why he had a trumpet on him.

As Reagan sat quietly reading a book, ignoring the mayhem erupting all around him, things got more and more out of hand. Obviously, some of the gin wasn't being wasted.

The flight crew, all Reagan fans, hung back as long as they could. Finally, as we neared Los Angeles, they pleaded with Reagan to exercise some adult supervision. With a look that gave much more in the way of sorrow than anger, he stood up, and made the universal "Keep it down, boys!" signal with his hands.

The reporters settled down; the water pistols were put away, and the cabin returned to normalcy. Reagan calmly went back to his book. I realized that night that he had probably saved the campaign from being the subject of a very embarrassing FAA investigation.

Fortunately, because the drunken miscreants were mainly reporters, the story of the Great Aerial Gin Shootout never appeared in any newspaper.

On November 8, Stan and I watched the election returns from our homes. We didn't want to intrude, take away any of the luster. We wanted people to think that Reagan had done this amazing thing on his own. That was our job. We were already too prominent. We were ready to fade into the background. Of course by then we also knew that we were through. It had been a once-in-a-lifetime event. After all, where would we ever find another Ronald Reagan?

In the end, I admit, I got it wrong. Reagan didn't win by a million votes. He won by 993,739, a smashing 3,742,913 to Brown's 2,749,174.

I was off by 6,261 votes.

But it was a terrific landslide: 57 percent to 42 percent.

And one of the people who joined the celebrations on election night was none other than Sam Yorty, still trying to stick it to his old foe, Pat Brown.

During his first press conference as governor, a reporter asked Reagan how he felt about being hanged in effigy at UCLA.

"I didn't know I would be so successful so soon," he laughed.

On the night of the inaugural ball, January 5, 1967, Stan and I went out with Bob Krueger and a few other guys for dinner to celebrate before heading to the celebration. They left the choice of a restaurant to me, which turned out to be a mistake on their part. I remembered a very high-class Hawaiian-Chinese place in Sacramento I used to go to years before. When the food arrived, we soon realize the place was under new, worse management and had fallen on hard times.

"That's okay," Krueger said graciously. We were still floating from our candidate's victory; we were in Sacramento to celebrate that victory, and even the worst pupu platter on the West Coast wasn't going to dampen our spirits. Besides, Stan got to order one of his beloved umbrella drinks, pronouncing it to be to his satisfaction.

After dining (if you could call it that), we headed to the ball, which was held in a gigantic tent. Unfortunately, it was a bitterly cold night and the staff had to bring in extra heaters, which at first had little effect. I remember seeing Jack Benny, who was then in his seventies, shivering as he sat at a table trying to keep warm. He wasn't the only one: A lot of the Hollywood A-list crowd had come to celebrate the victory of their old pal. I spotted William Holden, Robert Taylor, Chuck Connors, Buddy Ebsen.

They were all shivering.

Ron and Nancy, however, were immune to the weather. They were bride and groom, gliding across the dance floor. Freddie Martin was up on the bandstand, the same bandleader Stan had played for all those years ago. Reagan asked Stan to play again.

"Just one set," he said when Stan appeared reluctant.

Stan, like any good musician, always carried his mouthpiece, so he got on stage, picked up a trombone, bowed to his old bandleader, and played an old favorite, "I'll Be Seeing You."

It was, of course, our swan song. We already knew we were gone. Salvatori had told us. We could stay with the team but only under the supervision of Phil Battaglia, who was going to be Reagan's chief of staff. So, we were, in effect, fired.

We weren't around when, less than a year later, Battaglia quietly resigned in what Nofziger called in his memoirs the "Sacramento Daisy Chain" scandal. It certainly didn't help, but ultimately I don't think that's what caused his downfall.

Battaglia brought along several of his bright young men to serve alongside him. His big problem was that the efficiency and effectiveness that had marked his tenure as campaign manager seemed to desert him. His many absences from cabinet meetings—a no-show at eighteen of twenty-four meetings in May and June of '67—unsettled Bill Clark, the cabinet secretary. There were complaints about arrogance, manipulation of the staff, abuse of authority. When Reagan was shown an in-house report on Battaglia and his alleged shenanigans, Battaglia had no one to defend him.

Reagan, after working so many years in Hollywood, didn't care what people did consensually in their private lives. In fact, in 1978, when he was gearing up to run for president, he spoke out against the so-called Briggs Initiative in California that would have barred gay men and lesbians from teaching in public schools. "Whatever else it is, homosexuality is not a contagious disease like the measles," he wrote in a powerful editorial credited with defeating the initiative. "Prevailing scientific opinion is that an individual's sexuality is determined at a very early age and that a child's teachers do not really influence this."

In 1967, though—before the Stonewall riots in New York City, remember—the Battaglia imbroglio was something else. It was the kind of story that could undermine Reagan politically, doom him to one term in Sacramento, and quench forever any ambitions he had for the future. Battaglia and another aide decided to resign, and he returned to the private practice of law. Drew Pearson, the powerful syndicated columnist, however, published a column about the so-called "homosexual ring" operating out of Reagan's office, exaggerating the findings of the in-house investigation. Those of a cynical turn of mind suggested that the publicity was engineered to cut the legs off any presidential plans Reagan might be harboring for 1968.

When Stan and I, out of Sacramento and getting on with BASICO and our lives, read about it, we raised our eyebrows a little, then shrugged. We had tried to warn Henry Salvatori. But we preferred to remember the inaugural ball when Stan played with Freddy Martin and Reagan took us aside and thanked us, saying that he couldn't have done it without us, that he would never forget those three days in Malibu.

December 1, 1966

Dr. Stanley C. Plog and Dr. Stanley Holden
President
Basico
8155 Van Nuys Boulevard
Panorama City, California 91402

Dear Stan and Ken:

I'm later than I should be with this, but I want you to know how very much I enjoyed our relationship and how grateful I am to both of you for all that you did. I know that my homework on all of your good findings was a major factor in what finally happened. I would have been lost without the sound factual material you provided.

I hope our paths will cross many times in the future, and again I want you to know how deeply grateful I am. Nancy joins me in best regards to both of you, and we both say thanks again.

Sincerely,

Ronald Reagan

RR:kd

RECEIVED
DEC - 1966

BEHAVIOR SCIENCE CORP.

Governor-Elect Ronald Reagan's thank-you note to Stan and me, shortly after the election. His thanks meant the world to us then and still does.

EPILOGUE

Afterward came the inevitable post-election letdown. We were still young—I was thirty-seven, Stan thirty-four—but after sailing on that pirate ship it was hard to get excited about CEO evaluations. We were still in a daze. We had won our battle, proved our point. And now . . .

Now what?

We still had a business to run. Chuck Connors made a few tentative inquiries; maybe he was getting the political bug, but then he decided not to run. We had a contract with Sam Yorty, Pat Brown's old foe, who was thinking of running for the US Senate. Stan did great work researching the issues Yorty could use in his race. But Yorty's close associates were the classic cigar-smoking political "experts," and they weren't interested in this new-fangled approach to politics. They scoffed at Stan's suggestions, and we parted ways. A few other politicians sniffed around, asking if we were interested, wanting us to reproduce the Reagan magic, but in the end we weren't interested.

There was only one Ronald Reagan and only one miracle moment in Malibu.

Within a year we sold BASICO—to our old pal Bob Krueger—and went our separate ways. What had united us, our mutual thirst for conservative vindication, had happened a long time ago—or so it seemed. I wasn't done working for Ronald Reagan, though. On May 8, 1968, he appointed me to the California Board of Psychology, which keeps a keen eye on the licensing and behavior of psychologists and other mental health professionals—and contacts local district attorneys when we discover someone practicing without a license. I was

Stan and me (seated, he on the right) signing the papers selling BASICO to Planning Research Corporation. Dr. Robert Krueger stands on the left.

honored to serve my profession and my governor, and I held the post until June 30, 1971.

Julie and I moved to her native Hawaii, where I led a full and happy life, teaching, piloting commercial planes; I had long since qualified for my transport pilot's license and worked as a behavioral psychologist for the government in children's mental health. I was head of children's services, including psychological services to thirty-two public schools, in the Honolulu school district. I retired from the state mental health system after ten years. And, once again returning to flying, I was a captain for the Royal Hawaiian commuter airline. When Julie died in 1992, I moved to Chico, California, where I flew my own airplane and spent fifteen years in the Butte County Sheriff's Team of Active Retired Seniors (S.T.A.R.S.) unit. I was also a contract clinical psychologist with Butte County Mental Health and represented them at several Superior Court hearings.

Stan stuck to the private sector and became a very respected and successful consultant in the travel industry. He and his wife, Georgia, had two sons, Gregory and Stephen. In 2010, at the age of eighty-one, my friend Stan died.

Jim Gibson, our third musketeer, our motorbike-murdering madman from 'Nam, went on to become an executive at Atlantic-Richfield Oil Co. In 1984, in Washington for the second Reagan inauguration, he was involved in an auto accident that damn near killed him. He passed away in 2009.

Over the years, Stan and I had spoken about writing a book. The problem that always stumped us was that our business records for BASICO were scattered or destroyed. Neither of us realizing at the time just how close we were playing to history's open goal, we didn't keep a diary of our times with Reagan.

A lot of archives and books of that time mention our role, but we kept putting off doing anything, and our memories were getting a little rusty. After Reagan died in 2003, and then Stan seven years later, I felt the sands of this last opportunity running out. I am the last witness to that Malibu weekend. I, alone, know how that turnaround happened. I felt a tug of something like responsibility that this story should be told. Now you know it as well.

This, then, stands as my testament.

Time was when politicians came up through the ranks and learned on the job, through trial and error and without the benefit of scientific objectivity, how to do what Stan and I taught Ron in a few frenetic months. Political dynasties—the Kennedys come to mind—could also train the next generations from within, but this was the first time that social scientists did what we did on a first-time politico when so much was at stake. It's not too much to say that we changed the landscape by implementing sound scientific methods to achieve what's now known as media training.

On November 12, less than a week after the 2012 presidential election, the *New York Times* ran a story by Benedict Carey, headlined "Academic 'Dream Team' Helped Obama's Effort." In it Carey details how the Obama campaign availed itself of the help of the Consortium of Behavioral Scientists to swing the election its way. It was a much bigger operation than anything Stan and I did in 1966, but the basic goals were the same: Figure out what people think about your candidate, then nudge them toward voting for him and away from the opponent. "When asked about the outside psychologists, the Obama campaign would neither confirm nor deny a relationship with them," Carey writes, but "Consortium members said they knew of no such informal advisory panel on the Republican side."

Some things never change. Campaign pros still hate to acknowledge that the academics might know something that they don't. It won't surprise you to know that I wasn't thrilled with the outcome of the 2012 election—but I couldn't help but smile at seeing where the road that Stan and I paved has led. Maybe if Mitt Romney's people had given me a call, I could have told them: "Well, boys, here's how we did it for Reagan in '66 . . ."

Couldn't have hurt, could it?

ACKNOWLEDGMENTS

First and foremost, of course, Stan Plog, a great friend and colleague who contributed his immeasurable talents and energy to the cause, and Jim Gibson, a third musketeer. We fought the good fight. We were blessed to have such good friends, banded together, in such a noble cause.

Then, Ken Gross and Mike Neill, who helped bring long-ago events to life. My gratitude also to Al Zuckerman, an agent extraordinaire.

Finally, Ronald Reagan, who dropped into our lives so long ago, and showed us what was possible.

Appendix

"A TIME FOR CHOOSING"

Ronald Reagan's famous speech underwent many mutations and updates as he rewrote various parts of it to reflect changing times and realities. Here is the most famous version, delivered in 1964 on behalf of Barry Goldwater.

Thank you. Thank you very much. Thank you and good evening. The sponsor has been identified, but unlike most television programs, the performer hasn't been provided with a script.

As a matter of fact, I have been permitted to choose my own words and discuss my own ideas regarding the choice that we face in the next few weeks.

I have spent most of my life as a Democrat. I recently have seen fit to follow another course. I believe that the issues confronting us cross party lines.

Now, one side in this campaign has been telling us that the issues of this election are the maintenance of peace and prosperity. The line has been used, "We've never had it so good."

But I have an uncomfortable feeling that this prosperity isn't something on which we can base our hopes for the future.

No nation in history has ever survived a tax burden that reached a third of its national income. Today, thirty-seven cents out of every dollar earned in this country is the tax collector's share, and yet our government continues to spend seventeen million dollars a day more than the government takes in. We haven't balanced our budget twenty-eight out of the last thirty-four years. We've raised our debt limit three times in the last twelve months, and now our national debt is one and a half times bigger than all the combined debts of all the nations of the world. We have fifteen billion dollars in gold in our treasury; we don't own an ounce. Foreign dollar claims are 27.3 billion dollars. And we've just had announced that the dollar of 1939 will now purchase forty-five cents in its total value.

As for the peace that we would preserve, I wonder who among us would like to approach the wife or mother whose husband or son has died in South Vietnam and ask them if they think this is a peace that should be maintained indefinitely. Do they mean peace, or do they mean we just want to be left in peace?

There can be no real peace while one American is dying some place in the world for the rest of us. We're at war with the most dangerous enemy that has ever faced mankind in his long climb from the swamp to the stars, and it's been said if we lose that war, and in so doing lose this way of freedom of ours, history will record with the greatest astonishment that those who had the most to lose did the least to prevent its happening.

Well I think it's time we ask ourselves if we still know the freedoms that were intended for us by the Founding Fathers. Not too long ago, two friends of mine were talking to a Cuban refugee, a businessman who had escaped from Castro, and in the midst of his story one of my friends turned to the other and said, "We don't know how lucky we are." And the Cuban stopped and said, "How lucky you are? I had someplace to escape to."

And in that sentence he told us the entire story. If we lose freedom here, there's no place to escape to. This is the last stand on earth. And this idea that government is beholden to the people, that it has no other source of power except the sovereign people, is still the newest and the most unique idea in all the long history of man's relation to man. This is the issue of this election: Whether we believe in our capacity for self-government or whether we abandon the American revolution and confess that a little intellectual elite in a far-distant capitol can plan our lives for us better than we can plan them ourselves.

You and I are told increasingly we have to choose between a left or right. Well I'd like to suggest there is no such thing as a left or right. There's only an up or down—[up] man's old—old-aged dream, the ultimate in individual freedom consistent with law and order, or down to the ant heap of totalitarianism. And regardless of their sincerity, their humanitarian motives, those who would trade our freedom for security have embarked on this downward course.

In this vote-harvesting time, they use terms like the "Great Society," or as we were told a few days ago by the President, we must accept a greater government activity in the affairs of the people. But they've been a little more explicit in the past and among themselves; and all of the things I now will quote have appeared in print. These are not Republican accusations. For example, they have voices that say, "The cold war will end through our acceptance of a not undemocratic socialism." Another voice says, "The profit motive has become outmoded. It must be replaced by the incentives of the welfare state." Or, "Our traditional system of individual freedom is incapable of solving the complex problems of the twentieth century." Senator Fulbright has said at Stanford University that the Constitution is outmoded. He referred to the President as "our moral teacher and our leader," and he says he is "hobbled in his task by the restrictions of power imposed on him by this antiquated document." He must "be freed," so that he "can do for us" what he knows "is best." And Senator Clark of Pennsylvania, another articulate spokesman, defines liberalism as "meeting the material needs of the masses through the full power of centralized government."

Well, I, for one, resent it when a representative of the people refers to you and me, the free men and women of this country, as "the masses." This is a term we haven't applied to ourselves in America. But beyond that, "the full power of centralized government"—this was the very thing the Founding Fathers sought to minimize. They knew that governments don't control things.

A government can't control the economy without controlling people. And they know when a government sets out to do that, it must use force and coercion to achieve its purpose. They also knew, those Founding Fathers, that outside of its legitimate functions, government does nothing as well or as economically as the private sector of the economy.

Now, we have no better example of this than government's involvement in the farm economy over the last thirty years. Since 1955, the cost of this program has nearly doubled. One-fourth of farming in America is responsible for 85 percent of the farm surplus. Three-fourths of farming is out on the free market and has known a 21 percent increase in the per capita consumption of all its produce. You see, that one-fourth of farming—that's regulated and controlled by the federal government. In the last three years we've spent forty-three dollars in the feed grain program for every dollar bushel of corn we don't grow. Senator Humphrey last week charged that Barry Goldwater, as President, would seek to eliminate farmers. He should do his homework a little better, because he'll find out that we've had a decline of five million in the farm population under these government programs. He'll also find that the Democratic administration has sought to get from Congress [an] extension of the farm program to include that three-fourths that is now free. He'll find that they've also asked for the right to imprison farmers who wouldn't keep books as prescribed by the federal government. The Secretary of Agriculture asked for the right to seize farms through condemnation and resell them to other individuals. And contained in that same program was a provision that would have allowed the federal government to remove two million farmers from the soil.

At the same time, there's been an increase in the Department of Agriculture employees. There's now one for every thirty farms in the United States, and still they can't tell us how sixty-six shiploads of grain headed for Austria disappeared without a trace and Billie Sol Estes never left shore.

Every responsible farmer and farm organization has repeatedly asked the government to free the farm economy, but how—who are farmers to know what's best for them? The wheat farmers voted against a wheat program. The government passed it anyway. Now the price of bread goes up; the price of wheat to the farmer goes down.

Meanwhile, back in the city, under urban renewal the assault on freedom carries on. Private property rights [are] so diluted that public interest is almost anything a few government planners decide it should be. In a program that takes from the needy and gives to the greedy, we see such spectacles as in Cleveland, Ohio, a million-and-a-half-dollar building completed only three years ago must be destroyed to make way for what government officials call a "more compatible use of the land." The President tells us he's now going to start building public housing units in the thousands, where heretofore we've only built them in the hundreds. But FHA [Federal Housing Authority] and the Veterans Administration tell us they have 120,000 housing units they've taken back through mortgage foreclosure.

For three decades, we've sought to solve the problems of unemployment through government planning, and the more the plans fail, the more the planners plan. The latest is the Area Redevelopment Agency. They've just declared Rice County, Kansas, a depressed area. Rice County, Kansas, has two hundred oil wells, and the fourteen thousand people there have over thirty million dollars on deposit in personal savings in their banks. And when the government tells you you're depressed, lie down and be depressed. We have so many people who can't see a fat man standing beside a thin one without coming to the conclusion the fat man got that way by taking advantage of the thin one. So they're going to solve all the problems of human misery through government and government planning. Well, now, if government planning and welfare had the answer—and they've had almost thirty years of it—shouldn't we expect government to read the score to us once in a while? Shouldn't they be telling us about the decline each year in the number of people needing help? The reduction in the need for public housing? But the reverse is true. Each year the need grows greater; the program grows greater. We were told four years ago that seventeen million people went to bed hungry each night. Well that was probably true. They were all on a diet. But now we're told that 9.3 million families in this country are poverty-stricken on the basis of earning less than three thousand dollars a year.

Welfare spending [is] ten times greater than in the dark depths of the Depression. We're spending forty-five billion dollars on welfare. Now do a little arithmetic, and you'll find that if we divided the forty-five billion dollars up equally among those nine million poor families, we'd be able to give each family 4,600 dollars a year. And this added to their present income should eliminate poverty. Direct aid to the poor, however, is only running only about six hundred dollars per family. It would seem that someplace there must be some overhead. Now—so now we declare "war on poverty," or "You, too, can be a Bobby Baker." Now do they honestly expect us to believe that if we add one billion dollars to the forty-five billion we're spending, one more program to the thirty-odd we have—and remember, this new program doesn't replace any, it just duplicates existing programs—do they believe that poverty is suddenly going to disappear by magic?

Well, in all fairness I should explain there is one part of the new program that isn't duplicated. This is the youth feature. We're now going to solve the dropout problem, juvenile delinquency, by reinstituting something like the old CCC camps [Civilian Conservation

Corps], and we're going to put our young people in these camps. But again we do some arithmetic, and we find that we're going to spend each year just on room and board for each young person we help 4,700 dollars a year. We can send them to Harvard for 2,700!

Course, don't get me wrong. I'm not suggesting Harvard is the answer to juvenile delinquency. But seriously, what are we doing to those we seek to help? Not too long ago, a judge called me here in Los Angeles. He told me of a young woman who'd come before him for a divorce. She had six children, was pregnant with her seventh. Under his questioning, she revealed her husband was a laborer earning 250 dollars a month. She wanted a divorce to get an eighty dollar raise. She's eligible for 330 dollars a month in the Aid to Dependent Children Program. She got the idea from two women in her neighborhood who'd already done that very thing. Yet anytime you and I question the schemes of the do-gooders, we're denounced as being against their humanitarian goals. They say we're always "against" things—we're never "for" anything.

Well, the trouble with our liberal friends is not that they're ignorant; it's just that they know so much that isn't so. Now—we're for a provision that destitution should not follow unemployment by reason of old age, and to that end we've accepted Social Security as a step toward meeting the problem. But we're against those entrusted with this program when they practice deception regarding its fiscal shortcomings, when they charge that any criticism of the program means that we want to end payments to those people who depend on them for a livelihood. They've called it "insurance" to us in a hundred million pieces of literature. But then they appeared before the Supreme Court and they testified it was a welfare program. They only use the term "insurance" to sell it to the people. And they said Social Security dues are a tax for the general use of the government, and the government has used that tax. There is no fund, because Robert Byers, the actuarial head, appeared before a congressional committee and admitted that Social Security as of this moment is 298 billion dollars in the hole. But he said there should be no cause for worry because as long as they have the power to tax, they could always take away from the people whatever they needed to bail them out of trouble. And they're doing just that. A young man, twenty-one years of age, working at an average salary—his Social Security contribution would, in the open market, buy him an insurance policy that would guarantee 220 dollars a month at age sixty-five. The government promises 127. He could live it up until he's thirty-one and then take out a policy that would pay more than Social Security. Now are we so lacking in business sense that we can't put this program on a sound basis, so that people who do require those payments will find they can get them when they're due—that the cupboard isn't bare? Barry Goldwater thinks we can. At the same time, can't we introduce voluntary features that would permit a citizen who can do better on his own to be excused upon presentation of evidence that he had made provision for the non-earning years? Should we not allow a widow with children to work, and not lose the benefits supposedly paid for by her deceased husband? Shouldn't you and I be allowed to declare who our beneficiaries will be under this program, which we cannot do? I think we're for telling our senior citizens that no one in this country should be denied medical care because of a lack of funds. But I think we're against forcing all citizens, regardless of need, into a compulsory government program, especially when we have such examples, as was announced last week, when France admitted that their Medicare program is now bankrupt. They've come to the end of the road.

In addition, was Barry Goldwater so irresponsible when he suggested that our government give up its program of deliberate, planned inflation, so that when you do get your Social Security pension, a dollar will buy a dollar's worth, and not forty-five cents worth?

I think we're for an international organization, where the nations of the world can seek peace. But I think we're against subordinating American interests to an organization that has become so structurally unsound that today you can muster a two-thirds vote on the floor of the General Assembly among nations that represent less than 10 percent of the world's population. I think we're against the hypocrisy of assailing our allies because here and there they cling to a colony, while we engage in a conspiracy of silence and never open our mouths about the millions of people enslaved in the Soviet colonies in the satellite nations.

I think we're for aiding our allies by sharing of our material blessings with those nations which share in our fundamental beliefs, but we're against doling out money government to government, creating bureaucracy, if not socialism, all over the world. We set out to help nineteen countries. We're helping 107. We've spent 146 billion dollars. With that money, we bought a two million dollar yacht for Haile Selassie. We bought dress suits for Greek undertakers, extra wives for Kenya[n] government officials. We bought a thousand TV sets for a place where they have no electricity. In the last six years, fifty-two nations have bought seven billion dollars worth of our gold, and all fifty-two are receiving foreign aid from this country.

No government ever voluntarily reduces itself in size. So governments' programs, once launched, never disappear. Actually, a government bureau is the nearest thing to eternal life we'll ever see on this earth. Federal employees—federal employees number two and a half million; and federal, state, and local, one out of six of the nation's work force employed by government. These proliferating bureaus with their thousands of regulations have cost us many of our constitutional safeguards. How many of us realize that today federal agents can invade a man's property without a warrant? They can impose a fine without a formal hearing, let alone a trial by jury? And they can seize and sell his property at auction to enforce the payment of that fine. In Chico

County, Arkansas, James Wier over-planted his rice allotment. The government obtained a seventeen thousand dollar judgment. And a US marshal sold his 960-acre farm at auction. The government said it was necessary as a warning to others to make the system work.

Last February 19th at the University of Minnesota, Norman Thomas, six-times candidate for President on the Socialist Party ticket, said, "If Barry Goldwater became President, he would stop the advance of socialism in the United States." I think that's exactly what he will do. But as a former Democrat, I can tell you Norman Thomas isn't the only man who has drawn this parallel to socialism with the present administration, because back in 1936, Mr. Democrat himself, Al Smith, the great American, came before the American people and charged that the leadership of his Party was taking the Party of Jefferson, Jackson, and Cleveland down the road under the banners of Marx, Lenin, and Stalin. And he walked away from his Party, and he never returned till the day he died—because to this day, the leadership of that Party has been taking that Party, that honorable Party, down the road in the image of the labor Socialist Party of England.

Now it doesn't require expropriation or confiscation of private property or business to impose socialism on a people. What does it mean whether you hold the deed to the—or the title to your business or property if the government holds the power of life and death over that business or property? And such machinery already exists. The government can find some charge to bring against any concern it chooses to prosecute. Every businessman has his own tale of harassment. Somewhere a perversion has taken place. Our natural, unalienable rights are now considered to be a dispensation of government, and freedom has never been so fragile, so close to slipping from our grasp as it is at this moment.

Our Democratic opponents seem unwilling to debate these issues. They want to make you and I believe that this is a contest between two men—that we're to choose just between two personalities. Well what of this man that they would destroy—and in destroying, they would destroy that which he represents, the ideas that you and I hold dear? Is he the brash and shallow and trigger-happy man they say he is? Well I've been privileged to know him "when." I knew him long before he ever dreamed of trying for high office, and I can tell you personally I've never known a man in my life I believed so incapable of doing a dishonest or dishonorable thing. This is a man who, in his own business before he entered politics, instituted a profit-sharing plan before unions had ever thought of it. He put in health and medical insurance for all his employees. He took 50 percent of the profits before taxes and set up a retirement program, a pension plan for all his employees. He sent monthly checks for life to an employee who was ill and couldn't work. He provides nursing care for the children of mothers who work in the stores. When Mexico was ravaged by the floods in the Rio Grande, he climbed in his airplane and flew medicine and supplies down there. An ex-GI told me how he met him. It was the week before Christmas during the Korean War, and he was at the Los Angeles airport trying to get a ride home to Arizona for Christmas. And he said that [there were] a lot of servicemen there and no seats available on the planes. And then a voice came over the loudspeaker and said, "Any men in uniform wanting a ride to Arizona, go to runway such-and-such," and they went down there, and there was a fellow named Barry Goldwater sitting in his plane. Every day in those weeks before Christmas, all day long, he'd load up the plane, fly it to Arizona, fly them to their homes, fly back over to get another load. During the hectic split-second timing of a campaign, this is a man who took time out to sit beside an old friend who was dying of cancer. His campaign managers were understandably impatient, but he said, "There aren't many left who care what happens to her. I'd like her to know I care." This is a man who said to his nineteen-year-old son, "There is no foundation like the rock of honesty and fairness, and when you begin to build your life on that rock, with the cement of the faith in God that you have, then you have a real start." This is not a man who could carelessly send other people's sons to war. And that is the issue of this campaign that makes all the other problems I've discussed academic, unless we realize we're in a war that must be won.

Those who would trade our freedom for the soup kitchen of the welfare state have told us they have a utopian solution of peace without victory. They call their policy "accommodation." And they say if we'll only avoid any direct confrontation with the enemy, he'll forget his evil ways and learn to love us. All who oppose them are indicted as warmongers. They say we offer simple answers to complex problems. Well, perhaps there is a simple answer—not an easy answer—but simple: If you and I have the courage to tell our elected officials that we want our national policy based on what we know in our hearts is morally right. We cannot buy our security, our freedom from the threat of the bomb by committing an immorality so great as saying to a billion human beings now enslaved behind the Iron Curtain, "Give up your dreams of freedom because to save our own skins, we're willing to make a deal with your slave masters." Alexander Hamilton said, "A nation which can prefer disgrace to danger is prepared for a master, and deserves one."

Now let's set the record straight. There's no argument over the choice between peace and war, but there's only one guaranteed way you can have peace—and you can have it in the next second—surrender. Admittedly, there's a risk in any course we follow other than this, but every lesson of history tells us that the greater risk lies in appeasement, and this is the specter our well-meaning liberal friends refuse to face—that their policy of accommodation is appeasement, and it gives no choice between peace and war, only between fight or surrender. If we continue to accommodate, continue to back and retreat, eventually we have to face the final demand—the ultimatum. And what then—when Nikita Khrushchev has told his people he knows what our answer will be? He has told them that we're retreating under the pressure of the Cold War, and someday when the time comes to deliver the final ultimatum, our surrender will be voluntary, because by that time we will have been weakened from within spiritually, morally, and economically. He believes this because from our side he's heard voices pleading for "peace at any price" or "better Red than dead," or as one commentator put it, he'd rather "live on his knees than die on his feet."

And therein lies the road to war, because those voices don't speak for the rest of us. You and I know and do not believe that life is so dear and peace so sweet as to be purchased at the price of chains and slavery. If nothing in life is worth dying for, when did this begin—just in the face of this enemy? Or should Moses have told the children of Israel to live in slavery under the pharaohs? Should Christ have refused the cross? Should the patriots at Concord Bridge have thrown down their guns and refused to fire the shot heard 'round the world? The martyrs of history were not fools, and our honored dead who gave their lives to stop the advance of the Nazis didn't die in vain. Where, then, is the road to peace? Well it's a simple answer after all. You and I have the courage to say to our enemies, "There is a price we will not pay. There is a point beyond which they must not advance."

And this—this is the meaning in the phrase of Barry Goldwater's "peace through strength." Winston Churchill said, "The destiny of man is not measured by material computations. When great forces are on the move in the world, we learn we're spirits—not animals." And he said, "There's something going on in time and space, and beyond time and space, which, whether we like it or not, spells duty." You and I have a rendezvous with destiny. We'll preserve for our children this, the last best hope of man on earth, or we'll sentence them to take the last step into a thousand years of darkness. We will keep in mind and remember that Barry Goldwater has faith in us. He has faith that you and I have the ability and the dignity and the right to make our own decisions and determine our own destiny. Thank you very much.

—Courtesy of the Ronald Reagan Presidential Foundation

BIBLIOGRAPHY

Cannon, Lou. *Governor Reagan: His Rise to Power.* Public Affairs, 2003.

Colacello, Bob. *Ronnie & Nancy.* Warner Books, 2004.

Dallek, Matthew W. *The Right Moment: Ronald Reagan's First Victory and the Decisive Turning Point in American Politics.* Oxford University Press, 2000.

Evans, Thomas W. *The Education of Ronald Reagan.* Columbia University Press, 2006.

Kengor, Paul. *The Crusader: Ronald Reagan and the Fall of Communism.* Harper Perennial, 2006.

Morris, Edmund. *Dutch.* Modern Library, 1999.

Reagan, Ronald. *Ronald Reagan: An American Life.* Simon & Schuster, 1990.

Rosenfeld, Seth. *Subversives: The FBI's War on Student Radicals, and Reagan's Rise to Power.* Farrar, Straus & Giroux, 2012.

Schweizer, Peter. *Reagan's War.* Anchor, 2003.

Wills, Garry. *Reagan's America: Innocents at Home.* Penguin, 1987.

INDEX

Italicized page numbers indicate photographs.

"Academic 'Dream Team' Helped Obama's Effort" (Carey), 242
agriculture, 248–49
air travel, 102, 183, 233–34
Allyson, June, 18, 98, 104
Altschuler, Sid, 14
Anderson, Glenn, 89
Army Air Corps Motion Picture Unit, 20

baby-talking, 192
Bastiat, Frédéric, 146–47
Battaglia, Phil, 199, 211, 212, 220, 236–37
Bedtime for Bonzo (movie), 26
behavioral psychology, defined, 119
Behavior Science Corporation (BASICO)
　assessments and advice, 125–29, 131–34, 167–68
　candidate meeting and acquaintance, 139–48
　candidate performance training, 158–64
　consulting roles during campaign, 207, 233
　contact process and meeting, 120, 122–25
　contract and agreement, 134–35, 167, 223–24
　early consulting projects, 69, 121–22
　formation of, 66–69
　governor's job description education, 157
　influence, 211
　issue research and position development, 180–82, 184
　lint removal, 170
　organization of thoughts and issues, 149–55
　press coverage and criticism, 207–11
　sale of, 239, *240*
　staff, 170–72
Benny, Jack, 104, 235
Bergen, Edgar, 197
blunders, 112–14, 153, 173–79
Boddy, Manchester, 81
Briggs Initiative, 236
Broder, David S., 211
Brother Rat (movie), 18
Brown, Edmund G. "Pat"
　background, 73–75
　fair housing issues, 175
　political career, 71–80, 83, 84–90
　1962 reelection campaign *vs.* Nixon, 82–83, 91

1966 reelection campaign
  vs. Reagan, 90–95, 123,
  201–2, 221, 229, 233
bumper stickers, 183–84, 191
Bush, Prescott, 72

campaign consultation.
  See Behavior Science
  Corporation
campaigning
confidence development, 108,
  212, 217
  daily schedule descriptions, 183
  early weaknesses and
    criticisms, 110, 113,
    123, 126, 173–79
  endorsements, 197–98
  humor, 187–88, 194–96, 217
  polling vs. instincts, 190–91
  racism accusations and
    walkouts, 173–79
  rallies, 213–14, 220–21
  state touring, 102, 107–8
  stories and embellishments,
    188–89, 194–96, 228
  style and effectiveness,
    187–91, 194–96,
    217–20
  television appearances and
    blunders, 110–17
  UC Berkeley appearances,
    202–5
campaign management, 199,
  211, 212. See also Spencer-
  Roberts Consultants

candidate performance training,
  158–64
Carey, Benedict, 242
Chessman, Caryl, 77–79
Christopher, George
  campaign outcome, 221
  polling and feedback, 123,
    201–2
  as Republican gubernatorial
    candidate, 91–93, 173–76,
    179, 185–86, 218–19
  Spencer-Roberts assessments
    of, 103, 124
civil rights, 111, 173–79,
  199, 205
Cleaver, Margaret, 8, 13, 14–16
Communism, 9, 21, 22–23, 25,
  60–61
Conference of Studio Unions
  (CSU), 24–25
Connors, Chuck, 197, 213,
  235, 239
Conrad, Charles J., 115–17
Consortium of Behavioral
  Scientists, 242
Cordiner, Ralph, 29, 163–64
Cow Palace rally, 213–14

Dart, Justin, 226–27
Davis, Loyal, 28
Day, Doris, 19
DeFore, Don, 213
de Havilland, Olivia, 22–23, 24
Democratic Convention
  (1960), 79

Democratic Party
  California gubernatorial
    candidates, 90–91, 123,
    221 (*see also* Brown,
    Edmund G. "Pat")
  Reagan affiliation, 25–26,
    29, 32
Disciples of Christ, 7
Dixon High School myth, 189
Dobbs, Harold, 83
Douglas, Helen Gahagan,
  80–82, 105

Ebsen, Buddy, 213, 235
economics, 34, 146–47, 246
Economic Sophisms (Bastiat),
  146–47
education system, 203, 213
Eisenhower, Dwight, 82, 99,
  105, 179
elections, 221, 234
embellishments, 188–89
endorsements, 197–98
Eureka College, 13–14

Fair Employment Practices
  Act, 77
Firestone, Leonard, 226–27
Flynn, Errol, 18, 20, 107
foreign aid, 35–36, 253
freedom, 34–35, 246–47, 256
Free Speech Movement, 84, 87,
  190, 204–5, 213–14
Friedman, Bill, 107, 176, 177,
  178, 192, *208, 218*

Friends of Ronald Reagan, 32, 70,
  94, 103–4
Frye, Marquette, 87–88

Gates, Shel, 57, 59
General Electric, 28–29, 98, 163
Gibson, Jim, 171–72, 180, 182,
  184, 241
Girl from Jones Beach, The (movie),
  20, 26
Goldwater, Barry, 25–26, 31, 32,
  72, 99, 106, 109, 173–74,
  245–58
González, Elián, 35
government
  debt issues, 34, 112, 246
  growth of big, 112–13, 125,
    146–47, 149–50, 217,
    247–54
Great Depression, 14

Hale, Alan, 95
Halley, James W., 209
handshaking, 232
Harmon Gymnasium
  dance, 214
Hasty Heart, The (movie), 26
Hayek, Friedrich, 139
Heidt, Horace, 46
Herring, August Moore, 51–52
Hirsch, Werner, 210–11
Holden, Ken
  background and childhood,
    51–63, 141–42
  bumper stickers, 183–84

California Board of Psychology
appointments, 239–40
with campaign team, *218*
consulting businesses of, 66–69
(*see also* Behavior Science
Corporation)
contract renegotiations,
223–26
with Plog, *41*
with Plog and Krueger, *240*
Plog's first meeting with, 42
post-campaign life, 239–40
press coverage and criticism,
209–10
at press event, *178*
Reagan's speech, 33–38
Reagan's thank-you note
to, *238*
at UCLA, 39–40, 42, 63–64
wife and family, 63, 240
Hollywood Independent
Citizens Committee of Arts,
Sciences and Professions
(HICCASP), 22–24
homosexuality, 236–37
housing, fair, 174–75, 249
humor, 95, 103, 160, 187–88,
194–96, 217, 232
Humphrey, Hubert, 9, 25, 83
Hunt, Marsha, 104

inaugural balls, 235
International Alliance of
Theatrical Stage Employees
(IATSE), 24

John Birch Society, 105–6, 175,
197–98
John Loves Mary (movie), 26
Johnson, Clarence "Kelly," 41
Johnson, Lyndon, 26, 31,
72, 80
Jones, George, 34, 56–57

Kennedy, John F., 79, 81, 82
Kerr, Clark, 85, 213
Keynes, John Maynard, 147
Khrushchev, Nikita, 92, 257
Killers, The (movie), 101
King's Row (movie), 19, 20
Knight, Goodwin, 76, 117, 179
Knowland, William F., 76–77
Knute Rockne, All American
(movie), 19, 20
Korean War, 46, 62–63
Krueger, Robert W., 69, 120–22,
123–24, 235, 239

Lawson, John Howard, 23
LeRoy, Mervyn, 26–27
lifeguarding, 10–11, 16
lint removal, 170
literary allusions, 211
"Little Lindbergh Law," 77
Locke, John, 147–48
Love Is in the Air (movie), 17

Martin, Freddy, 46, 48, 235–36
Master Plan for Education, 77
McCarthy, Joe, 119
Meese, Edwin, III, 86

Meet the Press (television show), 197
memory, 184–85
mind-altering accusations, 208–9
movies, 17–20, 24, 99, 101, 162
Murphy, George, 105, 197
Murphy, Margaretta "Happy," 71

Nancy Hanks (ship), 57–59
National Association of Manufacturers, 98
National Negro Republican Assembly, 173–79
Neal, Patricia, 21
networking, 8
Neuropsychiatric Institute (NPI), 39–40, 51, 64–65
Night after Night (movie), 24
Nixon, Richard, 80–83
Nofziger, Lyn, 114, 115, *116*, 129, 133, 176, 177, *178*, *218*, 232

Obama 2012 campaign, 242
Old Guard, 72
Olson, Culbert, 76
Operation Boot Strap, 63

Palmer, B. J., 15
Palmer, Daniel David, 15
Parker, William H., 88–89, 90
peace, 34–35, 246, 256–58
Pearl Harbor, 56–57
Pearson, Drew, 237
Perry, Herman, 80

Planning Research Corporation (PRC), 69, 121
pledge cards, 191
Plog, Stanley
    background and early years, 42–51, *45*, 143
    with campaign team, *18*
    celebration dinners, 235
    consulting businesses of, 66–69 (*see also* Behavior Science Corporation)
    consulting projects, 122
    contract renegotiations, 223–26
    death, 241
    description, 42
    doctoral dissertation, 119
    family, 241
    with Holden, *41*
    with Holden and Krueger, *240*
    Holden's first meeting with, 42
    inaugural ball musical performance, 236
    post-campaign life, 239, 241
    press coverage and criticism, 209–10
    Reagan's thank-you note to, *238*
    at UCLA, 40, 42, 51, 65–66
polling, 123, 180–82, 190–91, 201–2, 227, 229
Powell, Dick, 18, 21, 98, 104
press
    BASICO criticism, 207–10
    candidacy reception of, 114

management strategies for,
159–61
pre-general election, 228
press conference blunders and
response of, 122–23
Q&A sessions, *208*
water pistol shootout,
233–34
press secretaries. *See* Nofziger,
Lyn
Proposition 14, 174–75
protests, student, 84–87

racism, 8, 111, 173–79
Reagan, Jack, 3–7, 8, 14, 18
Reagan, Nancy (née Davis)
at Cow Palace rally, 213
husband's schedule and
health, 182
at inaugural ball, 235
marital relationship,
192–93
meeting Reagan, 26–28
Nixon-Douglas senate
campaign, 81–82
Republican Black Caucus
walkout and support
of, 177
social life, 98
support of, 183–84
tea leaf predictions, 102
Reagan, Neil "Moon," 4, 5, 7, 8,
18, 162, 163
Reagan, Nelle (née Wilson), 3,
4–5, 7–8, 14, 18

Reagan, Ronald
acting career, 17–25, 28, 99,
101, 162
birth and childhood, 3–11
candidate performance style,
110, 113, 161, 187,
212, 217
children of, 19–20, 28, 101
college years, 13–14
early employment, 8–11
finances, 101
health, 134, 145, 175, 182–83,
198–99, 228
homes and property, 101
humor, 95, 103, 160, 187–88,
194–96, 217, 228
marriages, 19–20, 20–21 (*see
also* Reagan, Nancy)
memory skills, 184–85
military service, 20
nicknames, 4
personality descriptions, 4, 6,
7, 8, 17, 19, 37, 103, 104,
108, 158
photographs of, *116, 163, 168,
208, 218*
physical descriptions, 140, 151
political party affiliations,
25–26, 29, 31–32
radio sportscasting, 14–15,
16–17
religion, 7
social life, 18, 98, 104
Reagan Democrats, 97
Republican Black Caucus, 173–79

Republican Convention 1964, 31, 32, 72, 99, 109

Republican Party, 31–32, 69, 70–73, 99, 100, 120

Republican State Central Committee, 120, 121, 122

Roberts, Bill. *See also* Spencer-Roberts Consultants

  appearances and travel advice, 102

  behavior of, 212

  campaign management and Reagan vetting, 102–6

  campaign management reputation, 102

  contract renegotiations and reporting to, 223–26

  denigration of campaign consultants, 212

  description, 124

  political consultant meetings, 123, 124, 128, 135

  political consultant perceptions of, 132, 133

  Reagan support, 133, 198–99

  Republican Black Caucus walkout, 176, 177

  on Republican Party revival, 99

Rockefeller, Nelson, 71–72, 102, 106, 108

Rooney, Mickey, 144

Roosevelt, James, 22, 23, 24, 25

Rousselot, John, 106

Rumford Fair Housing Act, 174

SAG (Screen Actors Guild), 21–22, 24–25, 105

Salvatori, Henry

  background, 99–100

  consulting contract and renegotiations, 167, 223–26

  descriptions, 223–24

  gubernatorial campaign planning, 94, 99, 100, 102, 117

  perception of Reagan, 179

  political consultant meetings, 123, 124, 125, 128, 133–34, 135, 167–68

  political consultant perceptions of, 169

  Reagan television appearance, 110

Santa Fe Trail (movie), 20

Savio, Mario, 83–84, 203

Schary, Dore, 22

Schlesinger, Arthur, Jr., 22

Schneider, Taft, 94

Screen Actors Guild (SAG), 21–22, 24–25, 105

sexual misconduct accusations, 229

Shaw, Artie, 23

She's Working Her Way through College (movie), 26

shoebox clippings, 131–32, 148, 149–50

Short, Howard, 13

Smith, Adam, 147

Smith, William French, 94
Social Security, 36, 251–52
speeches
  for General Electric, 28–29
  Goldwater support, 31–38, 98,
    245–58
  of gubernatorial campaign,
    132, 151–52, 155
  speech writing process, 131–32,
    152–55
Spencer, Stuart. *See also* Spencer-
  Roberts Consultants
  appearance consultation, 187
  background, 102
  career, 191
  communications coaching, 108
  description, 124
  political consultant meetings,
    124–25, 135
  polling and position
    development, 190–91
  reputation, 102
  vetting of Reagan, 102–6
Spencer-Roberts Consultants
  authority requirements, 199
  campaign consultants and,
    211–12
  campaign contributions,
    108, 123, 169, 179–80,
    211, 229
  general election strategies, 227
  issues polling, 190–91
  political consultant meetings
    with, 124–25, 128, 135
  Reagan vetting process, 102–6

reputation, 102–3
support of Reagan as
  candidate, 123, 133,
  144–45, 168–70, 180, 181,
  185, 198
Stewart, Jimmy, 104
Storm Warning (movie), 19

Taylor, Robert, 235
television, 28, 32, 110–17, 197
Temple, Shirley, 26
Tennessee Valley Authority, 29
thank-you notes, *238*
That Hagen Girl (movie), 20, 26
This Is the Army (movie), 20
"Time for Choosing, A"
  (campaign letter), 106–7
"Time for Choosing, A" (speech),
  31–38, 98, 245–58
travel, 102, 107–8, 183, 192
Treaty of Beverly Hills, 24
Truman, Harry, 25
Trumbo, Dalton, 23
trust, 161–64, 177
Tuttle, Holmes
  background, 93–94
  campaign roles of, 102, 103,
    110, 199
  political consultant meetings,
    124, 125, 128, 133–34,
    135, 167–68
  political consultant perceptions
    of, 169
  as Reagan supporter, 93, 94, 95,
    98, 99, 179

unions, 21–25, 24–25, 60–61
United Fund, 28
University Consultants Inc., 67
University of California at
    Berkeley, 83, 84–87, 89–90,
    190, 202, 213–14
University of California at Los
    Angeles (UCLA), 39–40, 42,
    51, 63–64, 210–11, 235

Van Nuys rally, 220–21
Vietnam War, 34, 203, 204–5,
    214, 246
Voorhis, Jerry, 80

Walgreen, Charles, 8–9
Warner, Jack, 94–95, 162–63
Warner Bros., 17–18
Warren, Earl, 76
Wasserman, Lew, 162

water pistols, 233–34
water supply issues, 189–90
Watts race riots, 87–90
Weinberg, Jack, 85
Welch, Robert, Jr., 105, 197
welfare, 112, 113, 126, 154, 180–
    81, 250–51
Wilson, Bert, 13
"Win one for the Gipper" (movie
    line), 19
World War II, 20, 55–59
Wyman, Eugene, 209
Wyman, Jane, 19–20, 20–21

Yorty, Sam, 90–91, 123, 221, 235,
    239
Young Turks, 73, 92–93

Zanuck, Darryl, 101